# Through African Skies

Adventures of Bush Flying
in Missions of Mercy

## Ray Browneye

**BAKER BOOK HOUSE**
Grand Rapids, Michigan 49506

Copyright 1983 by
Baker Book House Company

ISBN: 0-8010-0853-0

First printing, October 1983
Second printing, June 1984

Printed in the United States of America

To my faithful, loving wife, **Anne,**
whose dedication as a God-given helpmate
contributed immeasurably to the service
described in these pages
and whose loving influence
continually enriched the lives of our family
and those among whom we lived.

# CONTENTS

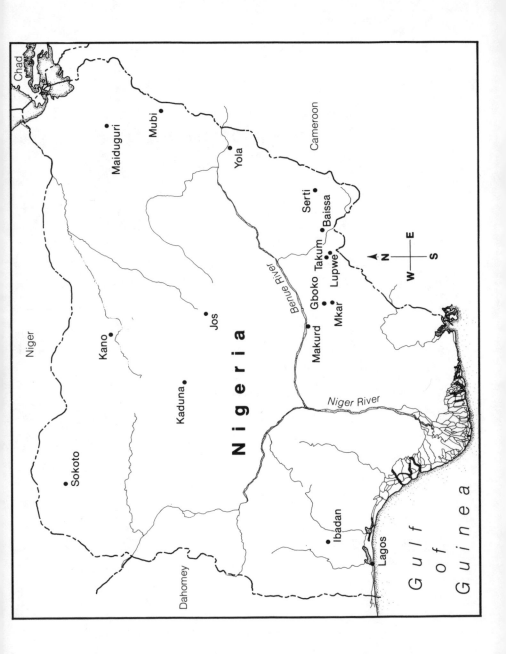

# The Problem and the Plane

Dawn stroked the sky with purples and pinks as I bumped along the dirt road in the mission's three-ton truck, trying hard to get to the Katsina Ala river in Nigeria for the first barge crossing of the day. People in the villages along the road began to appear outside their huts. Children and adults came out, and many waved as the truck passed. I returned their friendly greetings. It was a beautiful morning late in the wet season and, checking the time, I was encouraged about arriving at the river before the first crossing.

Almost an hour later the truck rumbled to a stop at the river's edge. The barge was gone! I looked across the wide river, then upstream near the riverbanks. There it was, moving slowly along the near bank of the river, but upstream from the crossing. I had missed it! I sighed so heavily it was almost a snort. Frustration and disappointment welled up inside. It was not the first time it had happened, and it meant a very long wait. My eyes dropped along with my spirits. I stood in the tall grass at the riverbank staring into the churning muddy water as it rushed by. I bent one blade of grass after another between my fingers, my hand doing one thing and my mind very far away, contemplating another. Then I looked up, shook my head, and resigned myself to the situation.

The wooden barge was just large enough for the one small truck it carried. It was being pulled upstream with a heavy rope laid over the shoulders of a dozen strong men on the top of the sheer riverbank. Progress could be measured in terms of feet per minute. After several hundred feet and a good half-hour, they stopped. Most of the men then scrambled aboard the loaded barge while the remaining few strained on the rope to prevent the hulk from submitting to the clawing current. Then they jumped on board from the steep bank, and the barge started down the river. The men picked up their long poles and plunged them into the water. The barge parted from shore, and for the first few hundred feet the poles reached bottom. The polers, spaced around the truck at the sides of the flat barge, synchronized their efforts and dug into the water in unison. When the fourteen-foot poles would no longer reach bottom they were used as semi-effective paddles. The men began a heavy rhythmic chant, and the battle of each crossing during the high water was on.

I watched with mixed emotions. High-water crossings were always fascinating, but I had left home at 5:00 A.M. and had driven fifty-seven miles to catch the first barge at 7 A.M. Another truck, however, was already there and waiting, probably since the previous evening; so the barge departed early. Now it would be half a day before it returned from the other side of the wide river. I was frustrated, yet there was something appealing and exciting about the men, with their bass voices, chanting as they battled the swift river. Rough-hewn manhood was evident in the bulging muscles and repeated plunging of the poles into the water.

The barge was now halfway across and going downstream rapidly, its human power working like fury in an attempt to get to the other side before passing the loading ramp. It rushed on. Still twenty feet from the other shore, it swept past the ramp. The poles plunged, the chanting was more powerful than ever. A half-minute later the barge brushed the grass at the edge of the bank several hundred feet downstream from the loading ramp. Then came the inevitable collision with the bank which sent the barge rotating clumsily end for end. A heavy rope was thrown to the waiting men on shore, and three others from the barge made the leap to the steep bank, clawing their way to the top. They dug their heels in the soft soil, straining at the rope. The barge slowed as every effort was made to stop it. Heavy soil broke off the bank and plopped into the water as the barge gouged into it while being brought to a halt. Then the rest of the polers wearily walked off the barge and began the back-breaking process of pulling the powerless hulk back upstream to the landing where the truck could be driven off.

The truck would be unloaded, another driven on the barge, and then the return trip to the side where I waited would occur. There was a lot more upstream travel involved. The crossing would be longer — much longer.

So while my fingers fussed with the long stalks of grass and my eyes at times stared into the water, my mind was thinking thoughts of how to get over, rather than across, that river. River crossings were only one part of the total travel picture and problem. Long trips, round-about trips due to lack of direct roads, urgent trips, medical trips — so many trips it seemed could be accomplished so much better with an airplane.

The process of obtaining an aircraft was long and complicated, but in God's own time it all did come about.

This book is not exhaustive in its description of the resulting flight service. Rather, it touches typical and special experiences, values, relationships, and people. Although their names are not mentioned, other personnel have and continue to render service of greater value than mine.

# 2

# A Tribute

There is a myth, or at least a half-truth, about mission aviation and missionary pilots which should be dealt with in an honest way at the beginning. The mission and the missionary are often portrayed as being dependent on mission aviation and the missionary pilot. That is true, but lopsided. Lest the complete truth be obscured, it is well to point out that the opposite is equally true.

Before the airplane arrives at its destination there is usually a flurry of activity that takes place on the ground in preparation. Cargo, mail, and luggage of every description is assembled. People get organized and prepared to go. They are transported to the airstrip or airport. After the airplane arrives, the cargo and mail must be delivered. The incoming passengers must be brought to homes, meetings, or places of work. The pilot is normally responsible to see that people, luggage, and cargo get on and off the airplane at the right place, but he is totally dependent on other people to work out the timing and execution of all the rest. Often sick or injured people are involved. They must be cared for in a special way. Family members going along with the patient must be dealt with. They are picked up from or delivered to a hospital, maternity unit, or dispensary. Long periods of time may be involved. Emotions run high. Physical and mental anguish are often evident. Adequate equipment for the task is not always available. But the job gets done. Without all that help, the flight service couldn't happen.

We call the hard-working people who do all these things "airplane chasers." The term is neither complimentary nor entirely descriptive. Whatever we choose to call them, they are at the very heart of the service, and we owe them a great debt of gratitude. We depend on them, and they come through with "flying" colors.

We also have "parts chasers." We don't call them that, however. The home office processes orders for and arranges shipment of a large number of parts every year. Without them we couldn't fly. That is dependence.

Also, mission radio operators handle, scrutinize, and relay all the airplane-related messages. Without the radios and those who operate them the aviation service would be in shambles a good deal of the time. We are dependent on communications and communicators to provide efficiency, and that is what airplane service is all about.

The aircraft mechanic makes an indispensable contribution to the flight service. He is responsible for the mechanical condition of the airplanes and, therefore, indirectly for safety in terms of mechanical function.

Then there are the nickels, dimes, quarters, and dollars that come from North America. Humanly speaking, it is doubtful that the service would have ever begun if one generous donor with vision had not offered to purchase the first airplane. Others took responsibility for the lion's share of later airplanes. Individuals, small groups, Sunday schools; everyone gave, from the young child to the elderly; on each we are dependent, and to each we are grateful.

And to those that pray, we owe a debt of gratitude that cannot be measured in money or material. God's response to them has been the gift of wisdom in operation of the aircraft, care over several million miles, lives saved physically and ministered to spiritually.

I have to write this book from my own experience and through my own mind and eyes. But please bear in mind that these flights involved many others.

3

# Beginnings

Should—or could—a relatively small mission in Nigeria, West Africa, have its own flight service? Over twenty-five years ago this fledgling idea teetered at the edge of the "nest," unsure of whether or not to launch itself into the untried air. But it did. It fluttered off and has, by the grace of God, continued to gain strength, stability, and purpose.

Miles traveled mean many different things. The four million miles flown by this flight service represent purpose and progress in kingdom travel in Africa, travel which is 60 to 95 percent faster than by surface and far less wearying to the traveler. More significantly it has been a means of accomplishing Christian work, alleviating pain, and bringing help to those needing it.

There are no first-class or economy sections in the mission planes. We have flown visiting church dignitaries from North America and Europe and people who had previously never even seen an airplane close by; and we have flown them together.

As pilots we have almost been wafted from our seats by the aromatic perfume of the lady who is determined to make the right impression on arrival in the heat. We have also been nauseated by the stench of burnt or ulcerated flesh of patients too sick to be concerned with more than clinging to life itself. We have had a few people die in our planes, but we have had many more who, humanly speaking, would have died had it not been for those planes.

We never intended the mission aircraft to serve as maternity centers, but on many occasions they have become airborne labor rooms, and on rare (thankfully) occasions, delivery rooms.

13

Severe tropical weather is usually temporary, but also extreme. The smooth, balmy air of early morning becomes the disturbingly turbulent, hot air of midday. The cotton-like, white clouds can in a short time be transformed into the dark, towering monsters we call severe thunderstorms.

The terrain over which these miles have accumulated year after year varies from semidesert to rain forest, from sea-level flatland to bulging hills and rocky peaks. The ground below is dotted with the grass roofs of compounds and villages, and, as development continues, by metal or concrete roofs, especially in heavily populated areas. There are miles of savanna bush or rain forest without a human inhabitant. The rivers and streams, which are so meaningful to the pilot as landmarks, wend their way among all these elements, lending character and at times great beauty to the panorama below.

It is strange in a way, but all those miles really mean nothing. What happened while flying them, and what happened on the ground prior to and after they were traveled, is most significant. Yet those miles very often formed the context for what did happen, and I want to express thanks to God for His unfailing care through each and every one of them.

# The Little Things

Actions, words, and often just the look on a person's face may betray the anxiety he or she has about flying. I try to keep such people as near to me as possible. In bumpy weather they shouldn't be in a yawing and heaving rear seat. Insecure people are better off seated where their fears can be talked about during flight. They are often a bit sheepish and ashamed of their own concern, so it is best to try to relieve them by explaining what to expect. Sometimes I've missed identifying the person who is anxious about flying and recognize the fear only when in flight I see giant beads of sweat rolling down the passenger's face and neck. (Airsickness will produce the same effect and add an ashen color.) This is especially true in the occasional bumpiness of light plane travel.

Some passengers, and this is particularly true of Africans unaccustomed to flying, will look for some form of security and attachment to either the airplane or the pilot. The seat belts are welcome. Clutching the seat ahead is not uncommon. A number of people who were frightened by motion sensations and who were sitting next to me up front, have firmly taken hold of my hand or forearm and have clearly indicated their level of tension by the tightness of their grip. A rough midday flight produces some very firm gripping. It can be a hindrance to have another hand tightly clamped on top of your own when flying the airplane. So I often say something in an attempt to reassure them and then remove their hand. Often the next big bump sends it darting back with a very firm clamp. Sometimes a person will grip my right leg above the knee. I usually ignore that, thinking that the person

15

feels uneasy enough without adding embarrassment. The idea is to get them to feel comfortable in the plane, however that might be achieved.

We all have images in our minds about missionary pilots and mission airplanes. Some of them are a bit romantic. We picture a sleek mission airplane soaring through the smooth blue sky carrying a critically ill national or missionary to the nearest medical facility where there is help and hope. This is fine and, in fact, often true. But a more intimate and complete picture is often quite complex and can be very "down to earth." Let me share with you what flying can be like at times.

We placed the patient in the right seat in the second row, reclining the seat fully. He was probably in his thirties, bearded, terribly gaunt, semiconscious, and incontinent. Precautions were taken to cope with that. He was desperately ill, and everything was done to get him on the way as quickly as possible. We normally have a brief prayer before departing and I believe it can be helpful, comforting, and a witness to the fact that the flight is more than help — it is Christian help, done in the name of Christ.

The loading had gone well, but it can often be an exhausting and sometimes exasperating task to get the patient, the people going with the patient (one of whom inevitably seems to have a baby on her back), the cooking pots, the food, clothing, and an occasional raucous chicken all into the plane. The temptation is to take a deep breath and pray, "Lord, somehow bless all this confusion," wipe the salty sweat out of the eye, and just GO. But it can't be done that way. The better procedure is to take it all in stride, do things deliberately and patiently, and try to have meaningful prayer with friends, relatives, and other onlookers before departure. We always tried to follow the latter procedure, but at times struggled with the former temptation.

A few minutes later we were in the air. It was only a twenty-minute flight. A radio message had been sent, so people would be at the destination, waiting with a car to take him to the hospital, only a mile from the airstrip. Everything was going like clockwork. If by God's grace the patient lived, he would arrive at the hospital in record time. But a few minutes out of Baissa, I noticed something was not normal. I was getting wet. There were no drops; just a very fine mist that I could feel on my face and arms. I searched for the source. Nothing was coming from the front, overhead, or lower air vents. I searched some more. Strange, but it seemed to come from behind. I had gone through heavy rain earlier in the day, but that should have shown up in the vent system long before now. I turned my head around and looked down between the second row of seats where another ventilator was placed. Liquid encircled it. It ran into the vent (which happens to be very effective in an Aztec) and was being blown up in a fine mist. I followed it back further. The liquid was trickling off the rubber sheet placed under our incontinent patient. Now it made sense, but I wasn't elated with the conclusion. I didn't really need a shower while I was flying.

I hastily reached back to change the creases in the rubber sheet on which the patient was reclined. That fixed the source of supply, but the "fine" shower continued. I tried to confine my breathing to exhaling only. We carry tissues aboard the airplane and I gingerly used a few to absorb the remaining urine around the ventilator while doing a shoddy job of flying. With a chuckle I reminded myself of my missionary calling and the fact that my number-one-concern was the welfare of the patient, not my own saturated self.

The patient, thankfully, did well.

The realities of running an air ambulance are not always pleasant. Body fluids, excreta, decomposed flesh, and bodies emaciated because of illness or accident are part of it. The marvelous thing is the way God uses the total ministry of doctors, nurses, pilots, family members, and colleagues (national and missionary) to meet both spiritual and physical needs. To be part of meeting those needs is a privilege.

I had a two-hour wait at our station called Serti (pronounced Ser-tee) nestled in a valley on the northwest side of the Cameroun mountain range. Bulging hills to the west rise to 4,000 feet within two miles of the station. The green carpeted slopes of the Filinga plateau rise 6,000 feet to the east. God's creative fingers touched and blessed this place with pleasant physical beauty. Both nationals and missionaries are attempting, by God's grace, to do something about the contrasting spiritual conditions that exist there.

Serti had a military camp a short distance from the mission station. As I walked across the compound, a soldier, who appeared to be in his mid-twenties, met me.

"Goot mauning, suh," he pleasantly greeted.

"Good morning," I replied. "How are you?"

"Suh, Ah no be well. Ah get pain in ma bones. Sometam Ah done vomit blood, suh. Ah want go wid you when you return Takum. Ah want go for hospital, suh."

"I see . . . ," I said thoughtfully as I tried to determine how to handle this. "Have you seen the nurse here?"

"No, suh. She no get chance see me," he continued in pidgin English. "She be too busy, suh."

Normal procedure was to go to Marge Kooiman, the nurse on the station, who was posted there specifically for maternity work (not general medical work), have her evaluate the patient's illness, and then make a decision about the necessity of using the plane. Marge was busy in the maternity unit. I was left to make this decision.

He looked well enough. Frankly I had doubts about his complaints, especially about the stiffness in his joints which he demonstrated with quite a bit of agility and dexterity. I was in no position to judge the medical aspects of his complaint about vomiting blood.

I agreed to take him along on the plane to the hospital. Experience had taught me to be careful. I had been wrong in making medical judgments on the basis of appearance before. It leaves one with a sick feeling later, and it is a very poor witness. In this case, however, I thought myself to be quite magnanimous, because I was quite sure there was really nothing wrong with him.

He went off to get permission to go from his superiors. Departure time arrived, and he was at the airplane waiting. He was as pleased as he could be. We spoke together for a few minutes before the flight and during the conversation he professed to be a Christian. I had no reason to question his testimony. He was the only passenger. We prayed together as we usually do before a flight, and then we were on the way. Since I thought he was on a pleasure trip anyway, I talked to him and identified points of interest on the undulating forested terrain passing beneath us.

My attention was drawn to leveling the airplane at 6,500 feet and correcting for the change in winds at that altitude. I established a new heading and settled down to flying the airplane.

About halfway into the hundred-mile flight I casually glanced at my passenger again. He was, from all appearances, contentedly looking at the rocky Fali hills north of Baissa. I looked again just a half-minute later. He looked as if he would explode! His cheeks were puffed out like a bugler's, and a fine stream of amber-colored liquid was jetting from one corner of his mouth straight on to the instruments ahead of him. His face was forward, but his frantic eyes met mine and desperately asked, "What do I do now?" I quickly slipped my hand around the back of his seat into the pouch for an airsickness bag. With his vigilance we caught most of it. He vomited heavily several times, then passed out. His head slumped forward, and the airsickness bag dropped on his lap. I caught it in time. By then I had punched on the auto pilot, so I held the bag to his mouth with both hands as there were indications of continued vomiting even though he was only partially conscious. Abruptly he returned to full consciousness. He became aware of the mess, and we made efforts to clean him up a bit. In a few minutes things were back to normal. I was relieved, but began to reflect on my medical judgment. Suddenly there was a repeat of the vomiting, fainting sequence. When he started I was ready, but when he fainted, I fumbled. The heavy airsickness bag distributed its contents all over his chest and midsection. I was really getting concerned about him. I held the retrieved bag to his mouth, and we got through it again. The remaining ten minutes of the flight were without further problems.

After landing, I asked him if he would like to wash up before going to the hospital. He enthusiastically agreed, and a few minutes later he was taking a typical African bath out of a bucket as though nothing had happened. The car from the hospital arrived, and he went to the hospital just as he entered the airplane except for some damp clothing which he had washed out. The interior of the airplane had suffered on this trip, and we cleaned that up.

Unfortunately it was often impossible to follow-up someone like this. The demanding flight schedule for the day didn't change. Often the last I saw of a patient was his or her entry into the hospital vehicle. That was frustrating, but often unalterable. There were redeeming factors, however. The hospital belonged to the mission and good care would be given. I was sure that a Christian ministry would take place with the patient. Sometimes I was able to go to the hospital later to personally visit the patient. Almost without exception I found them receptive and grateful. It was an effective opportunity for witness that came out of a helpful relationship.

The next day one of the doctors from the hospital was scheduled for a flight. When he arrived at the airstrip I asked him about my sick passenger from the day before. He said the young man died not too long after being admitted to the hospital. I was stunned. I thanked God for the patient's testimony.

A few scattered white puffs of cloud drifted far below us. At our level and overhead, it was clear and smooth. We passed over the Benue River while descending through 7,500 feet to our destination forty miles south. The river was carrying less water than it had the previous week. Massive sandbars were beginning to appear. They were wet and dark in color. During the next few weeks the top soil and silt would blow away and they would become tan and dry and clean looking. The Fulani with their cattle and the fishermen with their tiny shelters and drying nets would occupy them.

As I brought the throttles back to correct the increase in manifold pressure caused by our descent, the passenger next to me glanced my way and casually asked, "Do you ever get bored doing this?" I smiled at him and said, "No, I don't. Sometimes I get tired and once in a while I even get sleepy, but never bored." I wanted to ask him, "How could I get bored when there is so much to watch out there, and things to contend with in here?" but I didn't. His question was genuine and there was no need for me to be sarcastic.

I have been asked similar questions quite often but never while we were bouncing around in weather, or hedgehopping over the bush while coping with low clouds, or navigating in the reduced visibility of dry season bush fire smoke or dust haze. Neither has the question occured during equipment failures while in flight.

On one occasion a very dignified, elderly lady had come to visit her son, one of our medical missionaries. It was always great to see parents come to visit, and I enjoyed flying them and witnessing these reunions. We scheduled a flight for her, but the wet season plateau weather was behaving itself as usual. Thunderstorms were practically always part of the scenery in mid-afternoon flights at certain times of year. That doesn't reduce one's respect for them, but a pilot certainly learns to cope with them.

The enormous dark gray thunderstorms were starkly visible to the south, our direction of flight. The southeast held promise of better things with possible passage around the backside of the storm. The only way to determine if we could do that or if we would only run into more storms was to have a look. Neither foolish nor hazardous, it was just part of flying under such conditions.

My passenger was not totally comfortable in our "small plane." We departed, and she must have been very intimidated by the celestial scenery. It looked ominous. It was ominous. We flew to the east, working our way around the backside of the storms, allowing ample distance between ourselves and the weather. Outside of a few ripples and some light rain, which always trail behind thunderstorms, the flight was smooth. After we left the area and were well on our way to Gboko she turned to me and in total honesty inquired, "Mr. Browneye, do you ever go around those storms?" I had been complimenting myself about my generous and careful treatment of the dignified elderly lady, having flown extra miles and having consumed extra fuel all for the dear soul's comfort and peace of mind. I had to mask my disbelief and a strong impulse to chuckle. I was amused as well as a little frustrated by her evaluation of how the situation had been handled. I revised my facial expression, smiled at her, and tried to explain how we did, in fact, go around the storms, pointing out some of the differences between what we did experience and what we would have experienced had we taken a different route. She changed her mind to a certain extent about what happened, while maintaining her dignity and poise through it all. That, in spite of the fact that she was not comfortable when I looked at her instead of straight ahead where "airplane drivers" are supposed to look. I had to set her straight. Otherwise the good lady would quite likely return home and nonchalantly tell stories of flying through thunderstorms with the mission pilot in Africa. I have flown through a few thunderstorms, but never intentionally. It is a bad experience at best. I believe mission aviation has to defend itself against that sort of publicity.

Getting back to the matter of appearances, I believe most pilots try to be relaxed (not bored), and we hope we appear that way. Pilots can save passengers a lot of anxiety by observing some rather simple rules, most of which require a measure of self-discipline. A pilot should avoid craning his neck and bumping his head against the side window, looking for a checkpoint that should, but doesn't, appear. A darting, bobbing head with eyes in all directions, combined with abrupt, or even smooth banks to get a look at the ground, shakes passenger confidence, and rightly so. A pilot's head jerking from attention first focused on a chart, then to the ground, and again returning to the chart, with motion that resembles a nervous chicken feeding on corn, is unacceptable. Eye movement will take care of most of what needs to be done. But if a passenger asks the pilot if he has a stiff neck, you know he is probably overdoing it. Asking a passenger questions about matters related to navigation or position (except under the most abnormal conditions) is to merely reinforce any misgivings the passenger may already have about the competence of the pilot. Doing so with a grave look on your face will probably give the passenger nightmares after (and if) you arrive at your destination.

Regardless of what the pilot may suspect has happened after he hears a loud abnormal noise, he does nothing for the situation by facing his passengers with bulging eyes and a desperate, "What was that?" Rather, it is his responsibility to try to interpret it (Tommy may have dropped his toy airplane in the back seat) or calmly inquire about it if it is passenger related and unexplained. The pilot should know more about the airplane than anyone else on board unless he happens to have the mechanic as a passenger. In any event nothing helpful is accomplished by sharing his suspicions and interpretation, until they are verified or until some action needs to be taken. Then the passengers should be made aware of the problem and the method of coping with it. It is the responsibility and privilege of the pilot to keep problems to himself when it does no good for passengers to be aware of them and they can contribute nothing to their solution.

One of my worst performances in a stressful situation came to light after a flight was completed. We were taxiing to the ramp, and I asked the passengers to deplane as quickly as possible. I didn't realize it, but one of my passengers had been watching me rather intently, suspecting that something was wrong. Well it was, but it was with me, not the airplane. I thought I would explode and must have looked that way. When I came out of the rest room with a very relieved look on my face, Martha, who is a quiet and unassuming person, remarked, "I wondered what was wrong." I looked a little embarrassed as she continued, "I thought it was the airplane."

Speaking of long flights, right in the middle of one, and seemingly over the middle of nowhere, a curious (or concerned) passenger will ask with splendid composure, "Where are we?" Since there is little below except flat, uninhabited bush, it is a difficult question to answer with any precision. It brings home the point that there are a number of instances in which the pilot really cannot, from dead reckoning, answer that question because he doesn't know. That doesn't mean he is lost. When the question is asked between checkpoints, when there are no immediate visual references, it can be legitimately answered by citing what has already gone by or what will be coming into view ahead. Flying in remote areas leaves periods of imprecise position assurance. It is even more true over large bodies of water. If this kind of flying is viewed as a challenge in maintaining accuracy of headings, coping with crosswinds and weather, it will lead to maturation in piloting and a lot of satisfaction. Indolence, however, will lead to trouble, and remote area flying is very unforgiving of incompetence.

Some people have a real hang-up about riding in small aircraft. Of those, some adjust and others do not. I believe these attitudes are evident in two actual conversations that took place in Africa. One involved a person (who happened to be an African) who had never flown before. He was not apprehensive enough to refuse to fly, nor was he comfortable with the fact that he was going to fly in the mission's small plane. So he spoke to a friend about his apprehension. His friend, accustomed to flying with us, reassured him with the words, "Don't worry about a thing. They always pray before they take off and everything will be okay." He flew, and thankfully it was.

The other extreme, both in attitude and in spiritual approach, concerned a non-Christian European whom we were carrying because he was doing some technical work for the mission. Prayer was offered as usual before takeoff. After the "Amen," the passenger leaned toward the pilot, slowly turned his head, and within a few inches of his ear, quietly asked, "Is this crate really in that bad a shape?"

Whatever a passenger's attitude appears to be, the pilot can be assured that most people (if they are honest) would rather not be flying, and he does well to do everything he can to make the flight as comfortable and smooth as possible. Sometimes he must go out of his way to accomplish that.

I was flying a Nigerian lady, who was the director for medical

services, to one of the mission hospitals for an important government inspection. She was one of these impressive middle-aged
Nigerian women who have a certain no-nonsense attitude. They
have attained professional status, and they know it. She was on
time for the flight, weather was good, and things were going well.
We had several short conversations along the way, and she seemed
to be a very pleasant person. We began our descent. She became
very distraught. She mentioned the pain in her ears, and I leveled
off. I am sure she had read about neutralizing pressure in the inner
ear, but she had never had occasion until now to do it. I asked
her to swallow. She did, but it accomplished nothing. I asked her
to yawn. I am not sure whether it was self-consciousness or doubt
about the procedure, but she did it halfheartedly, so that was
futile. By now I could see good relations and the inspection falling
apart. She was hurting. She said she had a cold, so her problem
with ear pain was very understandable. I asked her to hold her
nose and blow, not letting the air escape from her nose or mouth.
She didn't understand the procedure. We went through it again,
and I demonstrated while we maintained altitude. On the next
attempt the pressure was relieved and she was most grateful and
pleased. But by now we were stuck with having to descend in half
the time which would increase the rate of descent and her problem. She managed well by repeating the procedure several times.
She was brought to her hospital hosts feeling just fine. At least
the outcome of her hospital inspection wasn't going to be colored
by a bad experience in the airplane.

# 5

# Traps

I recently interviewed two highly rated people for possible service as missionary pilots. Something struck me forcibly. They were both concerned about the type of flying they would be doing. Both had Airline Transport Pilot licenses, and both had considerable flight time.

There are some real differences between conventional flying done for business or pleasure and that done in the bush. Some people are put off by bush flying, branding it some kind of barnstorming activity, supposedly justified because it is for a religious cause. They are half, if not fully convinced that it amounts to little more than tempting God. Others view bush flying with mixed affinity and fear. Still others are very positive about it.

Regrettably, after an almost incredible safety record, mission aviation has in recent years had a number of serious, even fatal accidents. Thus the record has become mixed, as have people's attitudes. Regardless of how a person feels about mission aviation, there are certain areas in which physical laws and human weakness can combine and abruptly cut short a very helpful and fruitful aviation ministry in the bush.

The unexpected occurs at the inopportune time. A concrete example is the person who, sitting next to the pilot, finally loses the battle to airsickness while on final approach to landing. If the person being overcome distracts the pilot with an *urgent* request for an airsickness bag when the airplane is in that stage of flight, it can be disastrous. The simplistic answer is to prepare the passengers for such a possibility, but that is not always feasible when the pilot doesn't speak the passenger's language. There is also the problem of the power of suggestion with people who are not familiar with flying. To introduce airsickness bags and explain their use is, in some instances, almost tantamount to inviting airsickness along on the trip.

What should the pilot do if the situation occurs when he is fifty feet in the air on final approach? Simply put, he has to fly the airplane. Better a messy airplane, even a messy pilot (and I have been), than a bent airplane because the pilot was distracted. The airplane must have the management of the pilot when it comes in contact with the ground. Perhaps the descent, the deceleration, the turn onto final approach all combine to do in the person who has been fighting airsickness. I have had it occur a number of times. The first time the distraction took precedence for just a few seconds due to the misery of the sick person. I got back to flying the airplane just in time. Ever since that bad moment, I have remained alert to that trap.

During the dry and hottest time of the year, whirlwinds, which we call "dust devils," are a common sight in some parts of the tropics, especially if you are flying less than 3,000 feet above the ground. If the airplane happens to pass through one, there is an abrupt change in the altitude of the airplane, but nothing to really get concerned about other than passenger comfort and reaction. They are well named, however. They move along the surface resembling miniature tornadoes, pulling up sand, leaves, and other light debris, whirling it up to a thousand feet. They are the easiest to cope with in this visible form; but at times, like tornadoes, they don't extend all the way to the ground or they happen to pass directly over a paved runway where there is nothing to be pulled up from the surface. Then they are invisible. When "dust devils" can be seen and one "walks" out of the bush and crosses the airstrip ahead of the airplane on final approach, it is best to go around, give it some room and land after it has moved off. Close to the surface they are very capable of turning a light plane over or suddenly rendering control almost impossible.

For a number of years we could be just about certain that we were the only airplane in the entire southeast part of Nigeria. If there was another plane in the area we probably knew about it because it was an aircraft of another mission organization. Alertness to the presence of other airplanes was very low key. It easily stayed low key even when flying in areas where there could be other aircraft. Such an attitude needs watching. After months of seeing no one in the area, it was frightening one day when another airplane passed at right angles 1,000 feet directly below me when I had no idea anyone else was around. Thankfully we were both at the appropriate altitude for our direction of flight.

But airplanes aren't the only things flying in the sky.

Once we were flying about 6,500 feet above the ground when a solid thud against the windshield caught my attention. It was the termination of a very large bug. His remains splattered over the windshield in a cone shape several inches long. I never cease to marvel that large bugs can fly so high. More significantly, however, large birds fly even higher with the potential of tearing up the leading edge of the plane's wing, shutting an engine down, or smashing through the windshield. Tropical areas, especially those which tend to be dryer, have vultures in abundance. Over villages and towns, and at times over places miles from these villages and towns, big ugly vultures cruise silently through the air. I can't believe they do it with malice or much forethought, but often vultures, soaring higher than the airplane and in its line of flight, will partially collapse their wings and appear to dive for the plane. Descending to land at a larger town such as Kano on a hot day necessitates continual vulture dodging. It is especially difficult in descent, as the gray-black creatures are sometimes below the horizon and therefore more difficult to see. There are few flight operations with much longevity that haven't hit one. The sight of a large flying vulture population scattered through the sky produces an automatic rise in pilot blood pressure.

Watching an airplane speed over the ground at a low altitude is exhilarating to most people. The pull-up and graceful ascent are thrilling. That is called "buzzing." It is okay for airshows, and at times it is necessary for mission and other remote area operations to get attention for medical or other reasons. Frankly, I used to buzz lower than I do now. We all learn from our experience, or at least are supposed to. I found most buzzing was done unnecessarily low. There are a lot of statistics to indicate the truth of that. Unless the pilot is quite sure the person whose attention is to be attracted wears a hearing aid and is also quite sure the battery is run down, a reasonably low but safe pass should suffice. I once buzzed a station in order to have staff come out to the airstrip for emergency medical reasons. The only response we received was a friendly energetic wave from the person on the ground. Another buzz produced more energetic waving. I dropped a message. It was not seen and we got yet another wave. Frustrating as it was, getting lower (and therefore more subject to an accident) lent nothing to the effectiveness of the buzzing. The solution is that any low pass over any station should have a definite, predetermined purpose and a programmed response from those on the ground, or it isn't done. For a number of years a low pass over one of our mission hospitals, located a mile from the airstrip, meant we had a patient on board who should be picked up as soon as possible. "Gunning" the engines while making that low pass meant the situation was critical and every effort should be made to get the patient immediately. The cooperation and response were excellent. I shall always be grateful to those missionary wives, nurses, and doctors for the way they quickly appeared with a means of transporting those patients. Many of the patients were, and will continue to be, even more grateful.

There is another trap that seems to be the ultimate. I mention it because I, as well as many other mission pilots, have been tempted to enter its subtle clutches. What is written here is the only *fiction* in this book, but it describes the mental and operational process which has lead to some ghastly *non-fiction* in terms of mission aviation statistics. The deadly scenario has been repeated over and over. This is what happens.

The airplane arrives over its destination above a deck of very low broken stratus clouds mixed with some ground fog. The pilot has seen part of the airstrip through breaks in the cloud so he knows where it is. He also knows where he is in relation to it because of other visual references such as hilltops poking up through the cloud. There is no instrument approach. Due to the low cloud and ground fog there is no way to adequately see the airstrip on final approach. But the pilot knows exactly where it is. A low approach is made. Things don't go quite as he thought they would, and at the last instant he can't see quite enough to complete the landing. The pull-up is made. Just as he gets too far and too high to make the landing, the airstrip reappears directly below. The temptation wells up to do it again and push it a little farther because a little farther in the last instance would have made it! The cloud and fog aren't really that thick and it looks as though there may be some room between the base of the cloud and the trees, but there isn't a hole really big enough to get down through to find out. A second attempt is the answer.

Things get tense, altitude is where it should be, airspeed okay, gear down, partial flaps, props set. Everything is ready to "dump" it in if the strip is seen at just the right time, but the same thing happens. Just too late the airstrip passes underneath, but this time the attempt was even closer to being successful.

The pilot carries on an edgy debate with himself. He can wait for a while, holding in the area, go to an alternate airstrip and wait or give it one more try because he could see more on the last attempt. He has flown into the strip literally scores of times and is familiar with everything about it and with the airplane he is flying. He decides to give it one more try. Since there is almost no wind he debates about going in from the other end of the airstrip. It may be better from that end, but he says no to himself because the terrain is different from that direction. The conditions did seem improved on the last approach. The pilot, subconsciously congratulating himself on his conservativeness, decides to try once more.

From the small areas on the ground which are visible through the broken cloud layer he can almost be certain about his alignment with the airstrip. Everything is set up again. He has gotten himself into a mental attitude which says this *has* to work. This time the plane is flown just into the tops of the low cloud. He "knows" he is less than a half mile from the end of the strip. The slightly lower altitude this time will put him in a much better position to make the last minute transition to landing. A passenger notices the pilot is now a little uptight. He wants to get this thing done. Subtle pressures have introduced themselves, and the pilot has allowed those pressures to force him to push the limits.

There is no warning. Just a few feet ahead a blackish domelike form rushes at the airplane out of the misty gray. The pilot takes desperate action to avoid the huge tree by hauling back on the control yoke. He and his passengers are pushed hard into their seats during the abrupt pull-up. At the same time he shoves the throttle completely forward. The engine roars to full power. There is just one second of suspense, and the plane then impacts with the tree. There are harsh noises of rapid pounding from the propeller, high-pitched scraping, and metal bending. The plane shatters the upper, thin limbs of the tree and then, for a moment, is free again. It mushes along with its nose pointed high, desperately struggling for both airspeed and altitude. It wallows, seemingly suspended in the mist, then veers uncontrollably to the left and that wing drops abruptly as the plane stalls. It tumbles in the air and then hurls itself and its occupants into the dense trees. With horrible finality the plane falls sideways to the ground between two large trees. The heavy crunching sound is sickening. The forest is aroused. Shrill cries of birds in a hasty flight from the scene echo through the trees. Monkeys scold as they leap from branch to branch while stealing glances at the crumpled airplane lying on the forest floor.

Then everything is quiet — deathly quiet.

This is the way it will stay until the twisted wreckage is located. Why? Why?

Either because there were no predetermined limits, or they were not adhered to. No amount of regret will change the consequences. The bush pilot is often completely on his own in matters of judgment and discipline, two areas that demand careful and prayerful decision-making.

# The Inevitable

In 1958 when the mission was about to open Takum Christian Hospital in Nigeria, I remember Dr. Larry Den Besten making a statement to the effect that stepping up from a medical dispensary program with its limitations to a hospital and the treatment of more complicated and serious cases, was going to involve more deaths as well as greater preservation of life. It was inevitable. Similarly, it might be said that if the mission was going into long-term operation of aircraft, we could expect some trouble as well as fast and efficient transportation. Is that expecting too little of men's inventions? Is it expecting too little of God's care in operating them? In God's work, is it pessimistic to expect and prepare for the inevitable?

I believe not. But what is this "inevitable"? It is the high probability of eventual problems as a result of the electronic, mechanical, environmental, and judgmental elements in flying. Often a combination of these is involved.

I have seen God's very special care in many difficult circumstances. Situations were bad, but the decisions made in those situations, by the grace of God, were right. For that I am thankful, not boastful. I never felt that plunging blindly into dangerous weather because I was on a medical flight or working for a religious cause was worthy of the intelligence or training the Lord had given me. In fact, I am convinced it would have amounted to tempting Him rather than obeying Him. It would take incredible audacity to think that God would make it stay light longer so I could get a patient to the hospital before nightfall, or that He would remove the consequences of boring through a full-blown thunderstorm. On the other hand, it would be miserably unchristian to let a person die at an outstation because the margin of daylight left was short, assuming other flying conditions were acceptable. It would be unconscionable not to take every legitimate and conceivable measure to get a patient around prohibitive weather if what was ahead looked impenetrable.

Similarly, no amount of "faith" will ever keep the airplane flying without adequate fuel, maintenance, or airspeed.

To operate otherwise is to expect safety outside of obedience to the well-established, God-given, physical laws in nature which are applied in mechanical operation.

To expect great things from God in any of His enterprises is an act of faith. To disregard the God-ordained physical forces that work for you or against you in flying, in supposed dependence on "His" leading, is a perversion of that faith with deadly consequences.

That is not to say that all accidents are made up of such disregard. There are many additional reasons for them, but the temptation for abuse is present. The more urgent the flight, the more saintly the passenger, the more inspiring his or her task at the destination, the greater the possibility that irrational thinking will creep into the mind of the pilot. So while it doesn't happen often, there is a point at which the answer must be a polite and firm no to flying under certain circumstances. The yes can come when those conditions change. Still, the inevitable does happen—but not outside of God's providence.

It was about two o'clock in the afternoon. I was flying relatively low in the heat and blazing sun, making the twenty-minute hop from Takum to Baissa to pick up Dr. Art DeBoer, who was there on a medical visit. About ten miles out of Baissa I began my descent in the single engine Piper Commanche. I was passing through 2,000 feet when I suddenly saw two vultures directly ahead and all too close. They are difficult to see against the ground during a descent. I snapped the left wing down and the first one passed just over it. The second vulture slammed into the wing about two-thirds of the way to the tip, pulverizing the big bird, and ripping a large hole in the leading edge of the wing. It sounded like an explosion. It became obvious that the plane was going to continue to fly, but the wing skin had been ripped open and bent all the way back to the main spar. Distortion extended about eighteen inches on either side of the tear. The damage was directly ahead of the aileron. This muddled the airflow over that control surface, causing a lot of aileron flutter and jerking of the control wheel. I slowed the airplane to reduce the forces on the wing and prayed for wisdom.

I continued toward Baissa. The airplane was manageable, and I needed to sort out what to do about my passenger. A few miles out (two or three minutes after the bird strike) I decided not to land but to fly the plane back to Takum where we had the facilities to make the repairs. To land at Baissa, pick up a passenger, and take off before making the necessary repairs would have been both illegal and untenable. So I circled Baissa high, sending a message to them over the air-to-ground radio that I was going back to Takum without Dr. DeBoer—and why. Enroute I gained adequate altitude and then slowed the plane to a speed which could be used to go over the threshold at the Takum airstrip and still stop the landing roll in time. Everything indicated that the wing would still fly at an acceptable speed. I passed low over Lupwe which meant I wanted to talk to my wife, Anne, on the radio. She responded quickly. I told her of my predicament, asking for additional help in case of fire if things went wrong during landing. While she obtained the necessary people, I flew off to the southwest and held where I would not attract the attention of people near the airstrip. A circling airplane would attract hundreds. I certainly didn't need or want that complication on the airstrip. Anne advised me by radio when she and the others were ready to leave Lupwe for the airstrip, which was four miles away. I waited another ten minutes and then headed toward the airstrip. The landing gear extended normally, the wing flaps as well. These had been checked while returning from Baissa. I kept the speed up on the approach because the left wing was not as willing to fly as the undamaged right one. More and more control pressure was required to hold the left wing up as the plane slowed to a speed I could use for landing. On the short final approach, the wing dropped abruptly. It came back up, but required an abnormal amount of control movement. It was clear that I should not further reduce my airspeed. The plane slipped over the trees at the end of the strip and descended to a few inches above the ground, fast but level. I touched down, raised the flaps and braked hard. Dust boiled around the airplane as it decelerated to taxi speed before

reaching the end of the strip. All went smoothly, and we thanked
God.

News of the damaged airplane had spread, and when we returned home there was a large group of people gathered at the
house. We were grateful for the concern of the local people.

Dr. Art DeBoer borrowed a small motorbike and for several
hours made his sunburnt way back to Takum over sixty-five miles
of dusty dirt road. And he did it cheerfully, a blessing when we
had inconvenienced, rather than helped him.

I am even more thankful for the way the Lord prevented some
other decisions from turning into disasters. I want to share one
with you.

It was years later in the same area that we began a descent
into Baissa. I was taking one of our staff, Abe Vreeke, back to his
station. The descent was uneventful. Things were going as they
had hundreds of times before.

I put the landing gear control handle to the "down" position in
the Aztec and heard the normal noises as the wheels extended,
felt the drag, and then checked the three green lights, one for each
wheel. But I heard a different sound at the end of the cycle. I took
the handle and moved it to the "up" position to check the noise.
The landing gear came up partially and would not go back down
to the fully extended position. Several additional attempts to fully
extend the landing gear were futile. The hydraulic system had
failed. We had an emergency system, however, so all was not
lost—I thought. I felt it best to go back to Takum where the
landing gear could be checked and serviced after landing, so we
reversed course and headed for Takum. Enroute I prepared to use
the back-up landing gear extension system.

As we approached Takum I again pushed the landing gear handle to the "down" position. Through the cabin rang a shrill noise
which degenerated into a loud penetrating squeal as long as the
gear handle was in the "down" position.

I had already opened the small door on the floor below and in
front of the pilot's seat. It provided access to a small ring which,
when pulled, would cycle the landing gear down to the fully extended position. I got set for the pull, and pulled! It was met by
a sickening resistance and no action on the part of the landing
gear. I pulled and jerked until my middle finger was about to
bleed. It was evident that the back-up system wasn't going to

function either. I discussed the situation with Abe briefly. From his seat he could do nothing to assist. He just continued to watch this scenario unfold with increasing concern—and composure. Now there was little hope of getting the gear down at all. We flew on toward Takum.

We had to get the airplane on the ground one way or another. The prospect of a gear-up landing was not at all appealing. I decided it would be better to go to Jos, located two hundred miles northwest, for this landing. More room and smoother surfaces were the reasons. We struggled to gain altitude and slogged through the sky at a sluggish pace, with the landing gear partially down and without the ability to either raise or lower it all the way. I thought and prayed about the prospects and then discussed it with my passenger. It looked as though we would get the plane on the ground only with an intentional belly landing.

An hour and a half later I contacted Jos tower, asking for a SIM (Sudan Interior Mission) pilot to take a look at the landing gear as we passed low over the control tower. He did so. It was down far enough so that he really couldn't tell whether or not it was down all the way. Another SIM plane, which was departing Jos, flew close and underneath us. Neither could he tell whether the gear was all the way down. The facts were, however, that I did not have the three green lights indicating the wheels were down, and the mirror on the left engine nacelle indicated less than full extension of the nose wheel. I had to work with those facts. There was little left to do but land the airplane as gently as possible. I committed the inevitable to the Lord, and I am sure Abe did the same. I asked Abe to move to a seat behind the copilot's seat. That would move the center of gravity back somewhat while still providing him access to the cabin door to escape in case of fire. More important, it moved him back from the instrument panel in case of an abrupt stop. It also gave me access to the door to open it, without reaching around him. We would use the grassy edge of the smooth unpaved runway. I had to assume the main landing gear would collapse but couldn't be completely sure because the landing itself could pull the main wheels back into the down and locked position.

We approached slowly, and intentionally passed the uneven blacktop of the intersecting runway at mid-field. I closed the throttles and shut the engines down. The main wheels touched the ground. I felt the landing gear begin to collapse, and we sank slowly until the belly touched. The hissing and scraping sounds accompanying such a landing followed. The airplane slowed rapidly. The tail began to rise. The nose swung about ten degrees to the left and we slid to a halt. I opened the door and asked Abe to get out. I followed him, having shut off the electric and fuel. A fire truck sped to the scene. I met them and requested they spray nothing on the airplane as there was no indication of fire. Others came to the scene. We thanked God that there were no injuries and that the plane was only slightly damaged.

Later in the day, after informing the aviation authorities of the incident, we were given permission to move the airplane. We jacked it up, manually pulled the landing gear into the down and locked position, and taxied it back to the SIM hangar for repairs.

Yet, there was at least one redeeming factor in all this. It relates to something that happened as a spin-off.

Mrs. Lou Haveman, the wife of another mission staff member, tells it best herself. Here is what Jan had to say.

I was waiting in Jos for my child's birth, but it was still three weeks early. Someone mentioned that since the plane was going to Baissa, Lou [her husband] might be coming up a day early. After that we all heard that the landing gear was malfunctioning. Everyone was going out to the airport, and I wanted to be there too. Nobody really wanted me to go along because they thought Lou might be on the plane. I went anyway. As I sat there watching you circle and circle, I was getting more and more tense. My labor started and continued until I got to the hospital that afternoon. It was kind of funny, but when we watched you and Abe get off the plane, I said to Abe, "Oh, it's just you." I didn't mean to make it sound like he wasn't important — he just wasn't Lou!

Natalie was born the following afternoon. I was diagnosed as having placenta increta, an abnormal attachment of the placenta to the uterus. If I had continued to carry Natalie the additional three weeks, during that time my uterus would very likely have ruptured. Natalie would have died immediately, and I most likely would not have made it either. Dave Christenson, my doctor, showed Lou the uterus during surgery. It was paper thin and he said it could not have held up much longer. So going into labor at that time, I feel, saved us both. The whole two to three weeks before that I was having false labor. Dr. Christenson said the uterus was trying to sustain labor, but could not because one-third of it was already destroyed. It took that extra trauma to get me as far as I got. My labor stopped after getting to the hospital, but because my membranes had ruptured they had to keep me there and get the baby delivered. When they picked up erratic fetal heart beats which indicated fetal distress, they ended up doing a C-section. The whole process I believe was started with the Aztec malfunctioning. I don't think I would be sitting here writing this letter today if it wasn't for that incident. You just don't forget things like that. Especially when you feel that the Lord was directing each step of the way.

One of the greatest blessings we had in our later aircraft was weather radar. It should really be called weather avoidance radar. By "painting" areas of significant rainfall on the viewing scope it shows the pilot where the storms are and enables him to make a better judgment concerning the route of flight in relation to them. Unfortunately these things malfunction.

The radar had been working normally. It had proven its value time and again. When I was alone I had experimented by going into weather that looked questionable visually, but which the radar showed to be harmless. It invariably was. That builds confidence. But weather radars do deteriorate and may give a less than reliable weather picture because of a poorly functioning component, which doesn't necessarily cause complete failure of the unit.

I was returning passengers to the valley from Jos on the plateau. It was August. The plateau is hardly ever without some rain or drizzle on an August afternoon.

Light rain pelted the windshield from the high overcast as we climbed to altitude. Wisps of scud and broken low cloud blotted out parts of the terrain below. The weather was sullen, but not sinister. We passed through an increasing amount of cloud at our altitude. Shortly afterward we entered solid cloud with continuing light rain. I had a clearance for 7,000 feet and saw no reason to alter it. Several minutes of flying through the gray nothingness around the airplane passed. The radar painted nothing either. Suddenly there was an intense lifting force on the plane followed by a jolting loss of altitude with sharp jars and bumps. Lightning flashed. It had no shape or form. It just permeated everything around the bobbing airplane. Heavy but sparse raindrops spattered off the windshield for a few seconds. Then they lashed the rocking aircraft with indescribable volume. We had flown into imbedded thunderstorms which the radar had failed to display on its scope. The airplane shook violently. I reduced power to get as close as possible to what is called maneuvering speed. At that speed the airplane will stall rather than break up in midair if it becomes totally uncontrollable in severe turbulence. The airspeed needle swung wildly above and below that target. I fought for that speed, often having to temporarily surrender it because of powerful vertical air currents. The artificial horizon instrument, by which I was controlling the crucial flight attitude of the airplane, was blurred at times in the drubbing we were taking. It seemed miraculous that the engines continued to run in the cascade of water that the storm was hurling at us. It took intense effort to keep control.

Intentional descent was impossible. I was not worried about traffic, but I had entered the storm over the plateau. Often the base of the thunderstorm clouds over the plateau is too low to even think about descending below them.

The violence of the storm alternately decreased and then became worse. My passengers were praying. There was not a more appropriate thing to do.

Thankfully there was no hail, but we were in the middle of a mess and the only thing to do was to see it through. There was no way to back out. We went on with lightning flashing and rain battering the windshield. Suddenly there would be instant calm. Then another solid slamming of the airplane up or down, and the battle for control would resume. The radar was useless. I needed visual confirmation of the terrain below before I was willing to go below 5,000 feet intentionally.

A number of minutes later, after my passengers had bravely endured this repeated punishment, a small opening in the clouds indicated that we were over the extensive, flat Benue valley. I reduced power and began a descent. It soon became obvious that we should get out to the west. We flew through the driving rain and choppy air until we had done so.

Our departure from the violent air was as abrupt as our entry. All at once we were out and cruising on the smooth carpet of air ahead of the squall line. Thirty-five minutes later we landed at Gboko. I hardly knew what to say to my passengers. The radar had malfunctioned at a critical time, and we had flown into a line of thunderstorms. I thanked them for their genuine courage and patience. We gratefully acknowledged God's care through a bad situation.

I got back into the airplane and departed to pick up another load of passengers. I was beat. I felt much older. At the same time I was thankful to the Lord I could "feel" at all. Until the radar was repaired and tested, weather was dealt with visually.

There is something very important about these "inevitables" which I believe goes beyond the immediate. The value of, reaction to, and, more important, acquired judgment from these events cannot be underestimated. To be quite candid, I could easily have decided to drop the weather radar into the Benue River that day as I again passed over it. That kind of emotional reaction, however, is usually not valid. I believe the Lord has a monumental task in teaching us, and we should learn as much as we can from providential events which occur. They are there for our development, spiritual as well as mental and physical.

Now, lest you think that airplanes are bad and airplanes with weather radar are even worse, let's look at another incident.

Eventually the day comes when the pilot simply cannot go get the patient and bring him to the hospital. It doesn't usually work that way, but the inevitable sometimes gets complicated. The factors in this situation were time and weather.

I was working in the hangar at Takum at about 4:40 in the afternoon when my wife Anne drove up in a bit of a dither. She had been trying for twenty minutes to understand a message being sent from Serti over the mission radio. The outstation was one hundred miles to the east.

Weather was bad between us and Serti, evidenced by the anvils of towering thunderstorms which were becoming visible through the lower scattered clouds.

Static had made the message difficult to understand, but she did hear enough to establish the fact that Serti had a medical emergency and needed help. What its nature was or who was involved we didn't know. Anne had just gone through the frustrating experience of trying to communicate about something crucial on a low frequency system with a lot of static. She was plainly upset by it.

A glance at my watch told me that if we were going to do something, it needed doing very soon. I asked her to go to the hospital, which was about a mile and a half from the airstrip, to get a doctor to go along. We were not sure whether or not the patient could be brought back from the medical unit at Serti, or whether whatever had to be done could better be accomplished there.

I checked the Aztec and waited.

My thoughts turned to weather, to terrain, and to alternate airstrips in case we couldn't get to Serti. Part of the terrain between Takum and Serti is over 4,000 feet above sea level and prone to thunderstorms. There was one airstrip between the two stations. It was Baissa, a viable alternate. The question was, for how long.

I had decided to use the Aztec as it had weather radar installed, and it was much superior to the single engine Comanche in terms of carrying medical cases. Time was critical since it would be dark before 6:30 P.M. if we got any thunderstorms. The time needed to fly the round trip (seventy minutes), plus loading a patient with all that involved, plus likely having to deal with weather on the way, left less and less margin. At 5:05 P.M. Dr. Herman Gray arrived. He was doing surgery when Anne arrived and quite understandably couldn't leave immediately. I started the left engine as the car rolled up and the right one as he lowered himself into the seat beside me. We committed the flight and the situation at Serti (whatever it might be) to God, went through the check list, eased the throttles forward, and sped off the Takum airstrip.

Once airborne the weather situation became more apparent. Visually it did not look good. I turned the radar on. The picture it painted was also bleak. It was plain that we were not going to fly direct and maybe we weren't going to get to Serti at all. The radar painted a solid squall line with its bulges and irregularities running from northeast to southwest about forty miles ahead. It extended to the south as far as one could paint with radar or see with the eye. Hills exceeding 6,000 feet in that direction made it a poor choice as a way around weather anyway.

The squall line's position and direction of travel (directly toward us) eliminated the possibility of using the airstrip at Baissa as a place to land and let the squall go through before going on, so we headed northeast. It didn't really look any better, but it was too early to give up, and changes in tropical weather can occur rather fast. This took us to the edge of a range of hills which are heavily forested with rock formations jutting up sporadically. When we got closer to the squall line, we could see the lighter roll cloud with its swirling scud out ahead of the dark gray hulks with their stabbing lightning, and a wall of rain. It all verified what the radar had already told me. We were almost paralleling the line, occasionally turning toward it to get a better look at it on the radar scope.

Time was passing, and so were the options. Returning to Takum was out because the weather would probably get there before we would. I wasn't interested in long distance alternatives with impending darkness. There was no lighted airfield nearer than 375 miles and no navigation aid within 175 miles. A sound alternate was a bush strip to the northwest about seventy miles. There was no weather in that direction. That was realistic so we kept going. I was forced to fly parallel to the front of the massive line of storms. An attempt to penetrate it would be sheer nonsense. To go below it, close to the ground over that terrain, would be asking for another emergency in addition to the one we already had at Serti. I decided to go on for another five minutes. If nothing changed, we would have to give it up.

Several minutes passed. Then the radar painted a substantial break in the weather about fifteen miles ahead. The line continued on after that, but there was a definite possibility of getting through. The break became visible. It wasn't inviting, but it looked better than the torrents of rain and violence we had just passed by. A section of the line about eight miles wide had dissipated. We were at 2,000 feet and the ground over which the break would take us varied from 1,000 feet to just over 4,000 feet above sea level. We turned into the break, gaining the necessary altitude as we climbed toward the rain-soaked hills. I told Dr. Gray that the possibility of getting through had improved considerably. He acknowledged with a smile and a nod of agreement, and then returned to his preoccupation with the landscape below. He was an imperturbable passenger. I felt the break was safe because of the cloud type and action, absence of lightning, and adequate visibility. The forested hilly terrain had a sullen look under the heavy overcast. Wisps of low scud clung to the sides of the hills, and patches of cloud hid some of the peaks. We encountered moderate rain. The air was choppy but tolerable. Seven years and 5,000 hours of working this kind of weather without radar had taught me something of what to expect, and what had to be done in this kind of situation. I had to maintain sufficient forward visibility and adequate room to turn around in this hilly country. I had to avoid getting low near the lee (downwind) side of the hills and mountains. I had to have enough (but not excessive) speed to be able to use the maneuverability of the aircraft. These requirements were carefully observed as we picked our way through the rain, over and between the huge hills, and around the remaining clouds.

Once through the break and fifteen miles beyond, the weather improved. The terrain was more rugged, but the rain was light and the turbulence diminished.

Serti is approximately 1,000 feet above sea level. It is surrounded by hills which rise abruptly to 4,000 feet. You either "pop" over the top of it by maintaining an altitude which will take the plane over the hills or fly the valleys down to it. I did the latter in reduced cloud and rain. We touched down on the soaked strip, which is thankfully long enough to do a little sliding around without worrying about running out of room.

Bena Kok, the nurse, met us as we rolled up. The strip is immediately adjacent to the mission compound. She was very relieved to see Dr. Gray. The medical unit at Serti is a maternity center. Most of the calls for the plane are related to maternity work. With the medical problem being indefinite, Dr. Gray had taken a sterile pack to do a Caesarean section if necessary, as well as some other instruments and medical supplies not normally kept at such a small, limited medical unit.

The patient had been in labor for many hours. Normal birth for the child was not possible. There were other factors involved, including a history of ten pregnancies which resulted in spontaneous abortions, stillborn infants, or births in which the babies had died shortly afterward. This was the woman's first delivery under professional care. Bena described the situation to Dr. Gray. He listened, and then looked at me. "Will it be possible to get the lady back to Takum today?" he asked. The time was 6:04.

I looked up from my watch. "I'm sorry, Herman, but there is really no way to do it," I said. "It will be at least 6:15 before we get back in the air. That would put us back in Takum at 6:50 at best. That means darkness complicated by weather."

He gave me one of his wry smiles. "Well, I guess that settles that," he replied. "Bena," he continued, turning toward the maternity center, "let's go and have a look." They had their work waiting for them.

Settling darkness and light rain found me tying down the Aztec for the night. I prayed that things would go well for the woman and the child, and I am sure Dr. Gray and Bena asked for the same. I am also sure Bena had been praying for the possibility of help several hours before.

The small diesel electric generator at the station was started and the lights of the maternity center burned warmly across the compound. I was reading in the house in which we were to stay for the night. After some time passed, concern got the best of me. I walked across the wet grass toward the maternity center. As I got close I heard the cry of a newborn infant. When I entered, Dr. Gray was washing up and greeted me with a smile. He had delivered the child by Caesarean section. The woman had her first healthy baby. She would also hear the gospel daily during her stay and experience Christian care and love.

# 7

# Like a Vulture

We circled slowly and intently about seven hundred feet over the river, murky and broken by rapids and rock formations. The wide river was divided by two large, heavily forested islands with a rocky channel running between them. The channel contained the body of our friend and colleague, Bill DeJong.

It was Saturday afternoon when we received word that he could have possibly drowned. Those with him had narrowly escaped with their lives. Bill had been with Abe Vreeke, Dr. John Channer, and Dan Achtyes when their two canoes overturned while going through some very fast water in the Katsina Ala river. After it happened, Abe, John, and Dan had to shout to hear each other across the roaring rapids that had caused the upset. No one had seen Bill after he let go of the large boulder to which he was clinging. The three men decided the best thing to do was to obtain help in the search for Bill. Abe traveled the thirty miles to Mkar partly by foot (without the benefit of shoes which were lost in the canoe upset) and then by truck. He arrived shortly before 4 P.M. at which time the mission has radio contact between stations.

Abe's voice cracked a couple of times over the radio as he explained what had happened on the river. It was about an octave higher than normal when he emotionally responded to the question of Bill's welfare, "We don't know, but it doesn't look good." He then suggested an air search.

The location of the accident was just over halfway between Takum and Mkar, on the Katsina Ala river, and about ten miles south of the flight course between the two places. Several of us hurried to the airplane and flew to the approximate location, but

45

saw nothing. We went on to Mkar, picked up Abe, and returned to the area with him so he could tell us exactly where the upset had occurred. We saw the overturned and partially submerged canoes about a half-mile below the rapids. But we didn't see Bill. We scanned the rocks, the breaks between the trees, the water, anything that might have on it, next to it, or in it, a man clad in a blue shirt with the ability to wave, or hopefully somehow signal that he was all right or at least alive. But there was nothing. We flew over the site, upstream and downstream, low and then high, from every angle. Nothing. Then impending darkness drove us home.

The next day was one of hard searching by a number of missionaries and Nigerians on the ground, walking the banks and using canoes. The air search also resumed at dawn, and we received help from the United Methodist pilot, Vern Tryon, with their Cessna 206. We covered the river from the rapids to a point three miles downstream. The low flying with its constant maneuvering was fatiguing. We would alternately fly just above treetop level and then several hundred feet higher. The low passes gave us a close look; the higher ones, more time to visually investigate given spots in the river. It was important that the searchers in the plane did the looking and that I flew the plane as my primary task. There was a strong temptation to try to be both pilot and searcher. The low passes over the water and rocks, between the tall trees forming the borders of the curving channels of the river, demanded all the attention I could give them. Each pass had to be as slow as possible, while avoiding the danger of a stall. The passes needed to be precise in order to give the searchers maximum benefit and opportunity. Anything that had a blue cast was investigated more than once.

We took a break at midday for fuel. We also had to get rid of the mental numbness and near nausea from continual, intense searching.

We returned to the search in the afternoon, but the river stubbornly concealed its secrets. Then came the certain setting of the sun and the return flight to Takum fifty miles away. We reluctantly climbed away from the river with the empty feeling of even less hope for life and the haunting notion that his body was there — we just hadn't seen it.

During the same day a Christian Nigerian lady had come to visit

Bill's wife, Lois. Lois and Bill had visited that same woman a week earlier. Her husband had died unexpectedly. Now the two women sat together. The language barrier was present, but there was understanding.

Earlier that day Lois's colleagues thought it best for her to get off the station for a while. Just a short distance from the compound, they were met by about twenty-five Nigerian women who had walked two and a half miles from the town in the heat of the day to see her. Concern and sympathy flowed from them as they told her their purpose for coming. They prayed together. They all kneeled except Liatu who verbalized what they all felt in prayer. She stood, bowed her head, and pleaded with God, but committed the matter to Him. Lois was struck and heartened by their presence and prayers, by the kneeling black people who surrounded her with Christian love in the shimmering heat of the day along the dirt road.

Along with many concerned Nigerians and missionaries, Lois was at the airstrip to meet the returning planes. It was hard to look into her hurt, but hopeful eyes. My wife got out of the plane, walked over to her, grasped her hands, and confessed as kindly as she could that we had seen nothing hopeful. Fran Bratt approached her, put her arm around her in a motherly way, and spoke softly to her. Lois wept quietly. Fran conveyed what we all felt. Everyone was all torn up inside and feeling desperately sympathetic for Lois. She was very brave and very Christian, but some of her last hopes were languishing like the light of that day. She wanted so much to have some reason to believe Bill was still alive.

We prayed together, but it was even hard to know how or what to pray at that point; our hearts were full and empty at the same time. Words failed to find their mark, or failed altogether. But there was unity, even in silence — and there was love.

We wearily and silently pushed the airplanes into the hangar. The dull pounding of the diesel generator muffled the evening sounds of crickets and frogs.

Lois rode back to the station with other missionaries. She would stay with them for the night.

During the previous night (after the initial late afternoon search) in the privacy of her own soul, Lois acknowledged the real possibility of what might have happened. In the silence of the night it all seemed so unreal! She was here just as always. Friends and colleagues were here. But Bill wasn't—frightening and upsetting thoughts flooded her mind at times. Yet, there was still room for some reasonable hope that night.

Now an entire day of futile searching had passed, and little strength was left in the thin threads of hope that remained. The demonstrations of love and concern, the anxiety of waiting, the growing conviction that Bill probably was not alive, and the resistant hope that he was, all crisscrossed their way through her mind. But God supplied grace. There was no time when she felt that everything was going to come apart, including herself. That was not pride. It was the strength and assurance of God's grace.

A Nigerian friend came to our home that same evening to ask how the search had gone. He was from the Utur people, a small tribe that lived along the Katsina Ala river near the area where we had been searching. Africans who live near rivers acquire a great deal of practical wisdom about the waters that flow by them and from which they often derive their livelihood. Even the able Africans, however, do have an occasional accident in the waters they know so well. And the lesson they learn is the hard one we were facing. Water is powerful and deadly under certain conditions.

Adamu and I sat down together and talked. He wanted to know more specifically about the place and time of the accident. I told him exactly when and where it had happened. He was familiar with the white water there. His short, sturdy frame leaned forward in the chair he occupied. He was deep in thought and obviously making some calculations and some comparisons with past experiences. He commented on the bad stretch of river where the accident had occurred and then, in his thin, somewhat high-pitched voice stated, "You will see his body tomorrow." He said it with a concern that was genuine, but with a certainty that was upsetting.

I caught myself staring when Adamu broke into my thoughts as he politely, as Africans always do, announced that he should return to his compound. Customary exchanges of well wishing took place, one of which was the expressed hope that the other would sleep well. It almost sounded like hypocrisy, but based on the way I felt, it would be a necessity if I was going to fly the next day.

He left our home and walked into the night toward the seminary student housing across the compound. I stood there, half thinking, half watching his dim form disappear and then reappear as lightning began to flash in the east.

Then a bobbing flashlight beam appeared, coming down the path in front of the house. Anne was returning from another home on the compound. I waited for her, related what Adamu had said, and we discussed it. Sometime later we retired for the night and prayed together as we customarily do. We did so not being able to disregard the statement of Adamu.

Thunder growled in the distance and lightning pierced the darkness. Later in the night the storm crashed through and soaked the earth.

Weather was still foul the following morning. Vern, the United Methodist Mission pilot, was to take up the search while I made an early flight to Jos which couldn't be postponed. My passengers and I were to join the search on the return trip, which we did. But the air was so rough that I was losing my searchers to airsickness on the first pass over the river. Heavy rain battered the windshield. The low, ragged clouds seemed angry at our presence in their windy, soaking sweep over the drenched bush below. We were being jolted constantly, and all the yaw and pitch motion was taking its toll. I felt it was fruitless to continue until the weather moved through, so I continued to Takum with my passengers where Vern was waiting for weather to improve. Conditions were better to the east. Therefore I immediately flew on to Serti to pick up other scheduled passengers. We couldn't resume the search immediately anyway. Vern left for the river after the weather improved.

About an hour later Anne, who had the mission radio on, heard Vern call. He and those with him had located Bill's body.

As we climbed out from behind the Serti hills on our return to Takum, we heard the same message. After dropping off the passengers in Takum and picking up some fresh observers, we set out to relieve Vern who was circling over the floating corpse. We were concerned about the rising river due to the rain, and the possibility of the body being swept downstream. It was presently arrested by a rock and vegetation in a narrow channel. As we approached the area, Vern radioed the location. We sighted his circling airplane and flew under it, while listening to his description of the location of the body in the channel. A sick sensation passed through us when, from about five hundred feet overhead, we saw the blue shirt and then the blue jeans which covered Bill's spread-eagled body floating face down in the brown water.

I forced a verbal acknowledgment of what we saw to Vern and sincerely thanked him for his help. He turned north, and the blue and white Cessna 206 shrunk to a speck over the Benue valley and then disappeared.

We continued to circle monotonously, like a vulture. We were stunned and silent. The mission's General Secretary, Bill Van Tol, sat beside me. Abe Vreeke was in the seat behind him.

We looked down and were depressed by the finality of it all. The river had swallowed him and kept him for two days. Now we could have his body back — but not Bill. Faith in Christ, to whom Bill had gone, was the one thing that kept his death from being a total tragedy.

A hippopotamus lazed in the deeper water just upstream. It would be necessary to cross that area in order to retrieve the body. The hippo submerged, and then reappeared with regularity.

The people on the ground arrived after an hour had passed and made their way along the bank. We were concerned about their awareness of the hippo's presence. We scribbled a note, made a low pass and dropped it to them. They picked up the note and waved acknowledgment. They would take whatever precautions were necessary.

Nolan Vander Ark and Dr. Don Zielinga carefully got into an unstable dugout canoe with a Nigerian fisherman, who was nearby on the river. The long thin canoe left the shore and crossed the open water below the hippo. The Nigerian skillfully poled in the shallow water and paddled where it was deeper. About midstream in the river, they arrived at a point where jutting rocks and shallow rivulets made it more difficult to stay in the canoe than to get out. The Nigerian remained with the canoe and the other two men made their way toward the body, wading, slipping, and climbing through the rock-studded water. We indicated the exact location of the body by making several very low passes over it while they progressed. The floating corpse was impossible to see until they were within a few yards. They located the body. The sight shocked them, and there was obvious evidence of emotion, observable even from our distance several hundred feet above.

No attempt was made to lift or manually move Bill's body. Instead a rope was attached to an ankle. The floating corpse was then guided through the rocky channels, using the current to move it to a rendezvous with the canoe. It struck me strangely at first — and then as being uniquely respectful and gentle. It took considerable time to get back to the canoe. Emotions surged through everyone involved. Then the canoe with the three men aboard carefully guided the body to the shore from which they had come. When they arrived at the bank, others lowered a white sheet into the water. Bill's body was floated over it and lifted from its watery grave.

It was a silent flight back to Takum. The stark reality of what had been feared, hoped against, and at times pushed from our thinking, was now history. His young wife Lois had to be confronted with the final word. The body would arrive in Takum by road many hours later.

There was an ugliness to the flight that day which made it resemble the flight of a vulture. But beneath the appearance of things — and things looked incredibly bleak that day — there was a battered, but real faith: faith that through great struggle accepted God's wisdom and time for a man to die, for a young wife to be without her husband, for a missionary task to be without the missionary.

# To Communicate

One of the most frustrating things for an American pilot who begins flying in an African country, is the problem of communicating with air traffic controllers. This is especially true if the pilot has not been exposed to anything during his life except American English. The matter becomes less of a problem as time goes on, but it can be hectic for the uninitiated. The English varies from something sounding as though it came straight from London to an extremely difficult to understand brand of pidgin English. Fuel is often pronounced "foo-el." Fuel endurance is usually requested in terms of fuel on board in hours and minutes. It sounds more like "fool on board," and I have heard some rather confused Europeans and one American from Texas trying to figure it all out.

At other times the words are understood but the meaning or implications are not. One day a Pan American Boeing 707 was landing in Lagos. The crew member doing the communicating was one of those informal souls, in contrast to the usual rigid and formal aviation communications practiced in Africa. A visiting head of state was giving a departure speech on the international ramp. In addition to giving a landing clearance, the tower requested that Pan Am 707 keep noise to a minimum when taxiing in. The Pan Am flight acknowledged the first part of the transmission and then asked with near sarcasm, "What's this bit about being *quiet* when we taxi to the ramp?" In view of the size of the airplane his perplexity was understandable.

The strong tribal language accent of some Africans while speaking English, mixed with the variety of pilot nationalities with equally accented English, plus those drawling Americans flying around

53

for various reasons, can slow the whole system down due to the large number of "say again" occurrences. After two or three requests by the pilot for the message to be repeated, the temptation to just acknowledge with "Roger" can become rather strong. This can be dangerous and entirely inappropriate. One foggy morning in Lagos an aircraft had been told to report "southbound" from the final approach fix. However, southbound was pronounced "soutbound" and sounded like "outbound" to the pilot. This was an utterly incongruous instruction in view of the traffic, and the pilot thought the controller was being downright cantankerous, keeping him in the hold. I finally felt obligated to interrupt. Tempers were soaring, and traffic was going nowhere. I have had my share of these problems also. The only cure is exposure over a period of time, but it is always a frustrating and sometimes humiliating experience not to understand.

This applies to other areas of life as well, and sometimes humorously so. I needed a bathing suit when I was in Jos where there was a swimming pool. I bought one, only to find out that it had no supporter in it. I then proceeded to a shop where I thought I might find one. When I was approached by the Nigerian sales girl, I had some foreboding feelings of what this might amount to in the way of communications. I tried to look comfortable and asked, "Do you have any athletic supporters?" I received a puzzled look. I was into the conversation, and now I had to see it through. "Ah—um," I stammered, "I need an athletic supporter—a supporter." I tried to look expectant and confident, but her continued puzzlement only increased my discomfort with the entire situation.

"You want wat thing, suh?" she asked.

My courage was waning. I knew the whole affair was doomed, but not knowing how to back out, I stumbled on, "A supporter, an athletic supporter. It's like briefs — only — it's not briefs; it's a supporter." My voice trailed off.

Then came the crunch. "You are going to support wat, suh?"

I was embarrassed, but really felt like chuckling at this bungled communication situation. I didn't know what to do for a reply. Finally it came, "I—ah—I guess you don't have any," I mumbled. "Thank you anyway." I am quite sure that would take some kind of a prize in noncommunication.

One aspect of communications needs careful and purposeful predisposition. There is a temptation on the part of many English-speaking people (English being their first tongue), wherever they are, to judge the intelligence of others, whose first tongue is not English, on the basis of their ability to express themselves in English. It might be a measure of their education, but *never* of their intelligence. That is ridiculous arrogance of which many of us are guilty. Most English-speaking people would do well to learn a second language to appreciate the problems of becoming articulate in a second tongue.

A pilot is subject to this temptation because English communications with controllers and conversations on the ground with people working at airstrips and airports may be difficult at times. A condescending attitude will only show the pilot's lack of proper perspective in the total picture.

Those of us from the more industrialized countries have the same problem when it comes to using technological criteria as a basis, not for judging the technological status of a certain area, but rather, and erroneously so, to make judgments about the intelligence of third world people. There are no Ph.D.'s given in bushcraft. I have spent many days with people who couldn't read or write or speak a word of English, and who wouldn't know the difference between the tail and the wing of an airplane, but who were the finest people culturally, and had extraordinary learning and applied wisdom in the remote areas in which they lived. It is a rewarding experience to spend time with a man who can utilize so many of God's natural gifts in creation just as they are. It is even more rewarding when that is combined with the Spirit of Christ in the person. I believe it is very important to come to an appreciation of a different type of life than the technological, gadget-centered one in which most of us live. This is not to criticize technology, but to put it in perspective.

It is necessary to be able to communicate in the local situation in order to come to an appreciation of its people. For most of us learning a second language is a long, tough process, but it is worth every minute of the effort required. The lack of communication, while trying so hard to learn, is a great learning experience in itself. One aggressive lady, having just completed the course in the Hausa language in Nigeria and beginning to feel somewhat more confident about communicating, asked her Nigerian employee to bring her the *"ashannu."* She was asking for matches which is *"ashanna."* Since the word for cattle is *"shannu,"* that is what the employee heard. The African is polite enough not to break into roaring laughter (at least not to your face), so between the African's inability to fill the request and the language learner's inability to recall the right word, there is sometimes just prolonged silence. After that comes renewed effort and the same mistake is not likely to be repeated, but there are many more to be made.

The day one cherishes, in retrospect, is the one in which the response comes without thinking it through first, and without translating the words from one's first tongue. When you wake up in the morning, having dreamed in the language in which you have become fluent, it is a nice feeling. When you have not only caught the first and intended meaning of a discussion, but also sense what is under the surface and culturally related to those words, you begin to discount all the effort it took to get to that point.

The language-learning process has the immeasurable side benefit of enabling one to get into people's minds, and, in as far as that is possible, into their culture. You begin to make evaluations in terms of that culture rather than on the basis of criteria which have nothing to do with it. It makes possible the understanding of people, events, and attitudes which would otherwise be totally baffling.

# 9

# War and Clipped Wings

Mid-1966 found Nigeria plunged into civil war. There was little else on people's minds. Every conversation eventually got around to the fighting going on in the country. While there were no air battles, the war did take to the air in terms of transport and some bombing on both sides. The western extremities of our work bordered the area of fighting. The mission women and children living in Tivland were evacuated to the eastern area. Local Nigerian youth joined the army in large numbers. Some were not heard from for long periods of time. There were claims and counterclaims of victories.

The United States took a pro-Biafra stance and alienated itself from Nigeria (regardless of what may have been said officially). Nigeria turned to Russia for arms and armament. Russian Migs and Russian instructors were seen in abundance at Kano airport and, to a somewhat lesser degree, at other airports.

The country bristled with the military. Nigeria was at war with itself and attitudes reflected it. Many soldiers had minimal training. Foreigners, including missionaries, were suspect. After a number of years of almost total freedom to move about as we wished, there was a sudden change which involved numerous roadblocks, the necessity of carrying passports and residence permits, and explaining one's presence and purpose. It was new, and it was a shock.

We would not have been surprised to have the Nigerian government shut down our flight operation, but they didn't for some time. They did, however, restrict it.

The first flights under those conditions were traumatic. We had

57

always operated with a flexible schedule, and it was dotted with emergency medical flights which couldn't be planned. Now we had to report to the police, giving them a detailed copy of our flight schedule for the day. The day after this new procedure was put in force, a medical emergency flight caused a change in the schedule. As a result, I came into Takum without prior notice. I had a patient on board to verify the reason for the change, but I certainly upset things by the unscheduled landing and was the target of some very threatening words. It was evident that we were going to have to conform or be grounded. We tried, but tailwinds would make us early and headwinds would make us late. Security checks by the military at the point of takeoff would delay us, and we would get raked over by the military at the next point of landing for not operating on schedule. If an understanding officer was in charge, security checks went reasonably well, and no radical demands were made. If that was not the case, the situation could become very sticky and "harassment" would aptly describe what took place. I will never forget the occasion in which one police officer, whom I had known for a number of years, treated us as total strangers and acted like a military tyrant. I couldn't believe it. Neither will I forget other officers who were total strangers, who coped with unavoidable changes in our flight schedule with understanding and tact. Jos airport eventually greeted us with cannons leveled at us as we landed and taxied to the hangar. One of the most vexing things was being searched repeatedly when we arrived and departed. I often thanked the Lord at the end of the day for restraining my tongue when totally unreasonable demands were made. On the other hand it was war, and we could just be grateful we were able to operate at all.

Road travel was no better. Roadblock delays were common. That put more pressure on the aviation department. Therefore we had to fly more hours weekly than we were permitted to fly by mission regulation (related to fatigue and safety).

Medical emergency flights continued to occur, which either added to the confusion or enhanced the effectiveness of the work, depending on how one viewed it. At any rate, I landed one morning late in the week at the Gboko airstrip, where I had requested Rev. Harry Vanderaa, the General Secretary of our mission, to meet the plane. We were unavoidably late. The soldiers were not pleasant about that and showed their clear displeasure to Harry. He is a very conscientious man and a pastoral person. He heartily disliked the idea of a group of soldiers lying in the tall grass with rifles aimed at the incoming mission airplane. I had the benefit of not knowing they were pointed at me at the time. After we were on the ground (without being shot at), we explained our delay and apologized to a very irritated army officer, who was convinced our only intent was evil. Then I had to bring up the subject of flying overtime to a very distraught secretary. It turned out to be one of those tense, rushed dialogues, the unpleasant circumstances clouding the real issue. I accepted his judgment as he declared there would be no more flight overtime that week and later, in a calmer moment, wrote him a letter trying to convey its necessity.

There were two long years of this kind of operation with periods of lesser and greater tension. The war, however, moved southward and westward, away from the area in which we operated most. Getting permission for flights from the military became more routine. Relations with the military improved. There were only isolated incidents and rough spots. One procedure, however, didn't change and that was the relentless searching of baggage and cargo. We felt intimidated when the questions asked of us bordered on accusations. The apparent distrust reflected by the soldiers and the time lost in the whole miserable process was getting to me. As pilot I had to ask for special grace. I did learn something about patience, but I certainly wasn't among the most appreciative in the Lord's class.

Later in the war, a notorious Mr. Browne appeared on the scene. He was a Swedish mercenary pilot who flew for Biafra. I was uncomfortable about him. His resemblance to me in name and occupation was too close. He operated a B-26 bomber of U.S. manufacture, intended for use in World War II. But it was still around and he was creating a great stir with it, venturing far north within Nigeria, doing more psychological than physical damage. One afternoon he managed a sortie to Gboko in the heart of Tivland. We had a plane at the Gboko airstrip under repair and his attempt to destroy it came only eighty yards from a direct hit.

The bombs were homemade. Some were ineffective, such as the one which landed within one hundred feet of the airplane and left a crater about three feet in diameter and nine inches deep. The one which landed farther away dug a hole some six feet deep and fifteen feet in diameter. That would have destroyed our plane, so we worked feverishly on it, ferried it to Takum, and completed the repairs there.

Late in the war the military government grounded all civil aircraft including our own. The announcement was made without warning in the middle of the day. This precluded a flight out of Jos, where our Aztec happened to be while on a series of flights that day. The other plane was at Takum where both are based. We tried to obtain permission to fly the Aztec back to Takum, but that was not given for several months!

Then hope rose once more. A Nigerian Christian doctor with some military connections offered to help. Dr. Nuhu Andeyaba was a stocky man with a very pleasant disposition. He was also an extraordinarily able man and had been a friend for a number of years.

We agreed to meet and drive together to the army officer in Bukuru, seven miles from Jos, to see if something could be done about getting permission to move the airplane back to Takum where it should be.

Dr. Nuhu drove, and we decided he would be the spokesman. It would be better that way. Mr. Browne's escapades in the night with his B-26 bomber had caused all exterior building and road lighting at night to be banned until further notice. So we proceeded in the black of the moonless night, driving to Bukuru and then on to the other side of town where the barracks were located. No exterior lights were permitted for the military either. Therefore, we drove slowly along the front of the dark military camp wall, trying to determine exactly where we were. We could not maneuver the car into a good position to get a satisfactory look with its headlights. We decided we must be close to the entrance. Nuhu stopped the car. A soldier's silhouette appeared abruptly out of the black night. He thrust his rifle into the window opening on Nuhu's side and shouted belligerently, "Who goes — friend or foe?" He took us by total surprise. I couldn't see, but I think both Nuhu and I turned an identical grayish color at that instant.

Now occasionally Nuhu could have a mild problem getting words out as rapidly as he liked, and it could be exacerbated by tension. And there was plenty of tension here. I sat in uneasy silence.

Nuhu began: "Aahh — h."

Suspense.

Nuhu continued, "F-F-fr-fr-fr— Aah f-f-fri—END!"

The scenario paradoxically was as amusing as it was threatening. I don't believe either of us really thought the guard would shoot. I hurriedly confess, however, that I was grateful and relieved when he assumed a less menacing stance and withdrew the end of the rifle barrel from the open window.

Nuhu went on to explain our purpose and told him whom we wished to see. He also properly identified himself as well as me. The fact that he was a medical doctor aided immensely. We drove through the gate and were escorted toward the quarters of the officer. I turned to Nuhu, and saw his perfect white teeth in a broad smile. We chuckled together about our own surprise at the initial reception, but kept it low key. We were grateful to be on the way to see the captain.

Our visit actually accomplished little that night. It did, however, point out to Nuhu the chain of command through which we eventually obtained military permission to fly the airplane to Takum.

It had been five months since the airplane had flown. All civil aircraft were still grounded, and we had permission just for one flight. I wanted nothing to go wrong. I saw no need of doing a hundred-hour inspection on the plane, but did go through a long and thorough preflight inspection and again checked with the military. I taxied to the end of the runway and went through the check list and engine runups. Everything appeared to be okay. It was thrilling to think that we were going to get the Aztec back to base.

I advanced the throttles and accelerated down the runway to the east. The right engine began to surge a bit toward the end of the runway after I lifted off. It was too late to abort and the last thing I wanted to do was to have to land. The engine, however, continued to surge. I had no choice but to turn around. That was a tough 180 degree turn to make. I told the tower what my intentions were and why. They responded positively, but I was not sure what the military's response was going to be. I landed without any trouble from them and then went up to the tower to explain. The tower and the military gave me permission to take off again after the problem was corrected. I found the difficulty, corrected it, and a short time later was back in the air on the way to Takum, relieved and happy.

After five months it was good just to be flying. I gratefully acknowledged God's kindness, sped over the plateau, down into the Benue valley, across the river, and touched down next to the foothills of the Camerouns in Takum. The Aztec was back home. Grounded again, but home, and not to be grounded for long. The war ended two months later, and the burdensome restrictions and regulations were gradually lifted.

# 10

# The Journey of Manja

Tissa (pronounced Tee-saa) is a small village nestled under tall trees two hundred yards from the Donga River, twenty miles east of Takum. Its one-hundred-fifty to two-hundred inhabitants are Chamba by tribe, fishermen and farmers by vocation. The majority have tenaciously clung to their pagan ways in spite of serious efforts to reach them with the gospel. Small beginnings have been made, however. There is a nucleus of Christians in the village. Tissa's establishment, meanwhile, remains committed to and enslaved by pagan practice.

It is a picturesque place. In the wet season the river cascades over the huge rocks nearby. Inside the village the distant muffled roar is broken by a woman chanting as she grinds grain by hand over a dished-out rock. Raspy male voices filter from behind thatched grass partitions that separate the family compounds. A few malnourished dogs move from one compound to another in their restless and relentless search for food. Small bush chickens cackle and colorful roosters crow, almost symbolizing the village where they live with their small size but proud character. A few dirty sheep lie idly under the mango trees while several others probe the ground in the village and the surrounding bush for a morsel of food.

The sound of small children's voices breaks through all the other noises, sometimes with laughter which may quickly turn to crying. The rhythmic clack of the wooden pestle, being driven to the bottom of the crudely carved mahogany mortar by the strong arms of an adolescent girl as she pounds guinea corn, seems to say that life goes on as it has for so long in that little village.

Smoke seeps through the roofs of several huts from small fires under cooking pots. In the calm of the early morning the smoke moves slowly up from the roof. It ascends a few feet and then flattens into a thin wisp forming a canopy over the huts.

I have sat under the mango tree in the center of the village on a number of mornings observing all this while I waited for Manja or another hunting guide. I have asked myself questions about the apparent serenity, about the lack of all the pressures with which we from the Western world live. I admired the simplicity of life here.

Then a small child passed by and I had to ask myself about his distended tummy, his thin arms and watery eyes. Many of my questions have at least been partially answered over years of exposure to these people. The serenity is matched by poverty. There are hidden pressures of threats and curses that only come to light after an intimate acquaintance of long standing, and then I am sure, just partially. Human nature is no different in Africa's idyllic setting. At its depths it is sinful and needy. What human nature needs is love, hope, purpose, security, and most of all, God. Paganism cannot and does not provide that. I am convinced that real Christianity does. That is why I became involved in Christian missions.

I believe that a missionary, including one in a technical job, should also have a spiritual ministry if he or she is going to, in fact, be a missionary. This can be accomplished in a number of ways, the greatest of which is a person-to-person witness through lifestyle, coupled with a verbal testimony for Christ. There are additional channels.

Prior to our first contact, Tissa was just the name of a village along the Donga river and a place to hunt antelope. Harold Padding, the administrator, laboratory supervisor, and X-ray department supervisor of Takum Christian Hospital (if you want to mention technical involvement) and I originally came to Tissa to hunt. A few hours of sweating together in the bush with the local village people, however, revealed a spiritual need much greater than our need to hunt. So we tried to meet both, but ultimately spent more time with the spiritual needs of these people. Together and separately, we worked with the people of Tissa. Daniel Kukwe, a Nigerian evangelist, also became involved and local leadership began to emerge from Tissa itself. Almost two decades were in-

The faithful Aztec. It was flown a million and a half miles, almost nine thousand hours, over an eleven-year span.

Beautiful, rugged terrain along Nigeria's eastern border.

Medicine, literature, building supplies, mail, food—if it would go in, it was carried.

Loading an unconscious patient.

Over mountains and clouds.

Descending between the hills into the Benue valley.

Assisting a patient after arrival at the Takum airstrip, about a mile from the hospital.

The busyness of unloading and loading passengers and cargo.

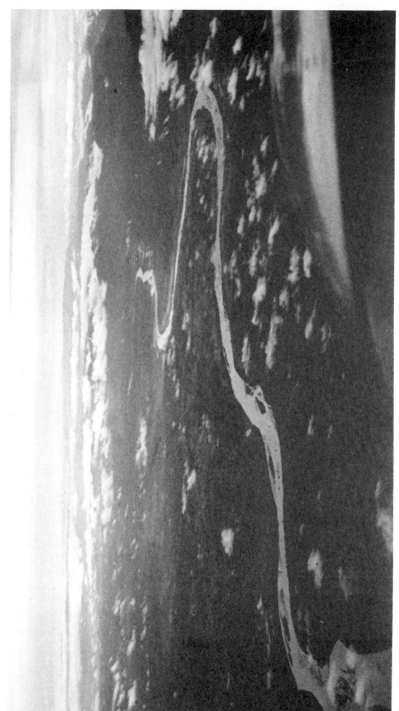

Passing over the Benue River.

An ill Fulani woman on her way to getting medical help.

Checking the fish traps on the river near Tissa.

The coastline of the Azores.

Marge Kooiman and I organizing a multiple patient load, all victims of a road accident.

He lost his leg, but his life was saved.

The Twin Comanche heading home.

volved. Sometimes it was disappointing, but there was always hope and new commitments. There were periodic baptisms. People found Christ in that pagan place. Manja was one of them.

He was a middle-aged man, rather tall and lean. His eyes were bright, and he had a ready smile. He had a distinctive crackle in his voice. He was a pagan and seemed to fit well into the establishment in the village. He was also a good hunter.

Over a period of time our relationship become more than the white man – black tracker sort of image that people have. He was a pagan friend. Out of courtesy he and other leaders in the village would attend the worship services which had begun. We talked to Manja about God while hunting in the bush together. Then one circumstance in particular brought all our talk to a head. I had shot at a large crocodile in the river. The water was almost motionless and quite deep. The crocodile had disappeared under the surface after the shot, but the question of his being dead or alive was unanswered.

Manja promptly removed two leather-bound bracelets from a handmade "belt" he had tied around his waist. He slipped them on his wrists and said in Hausa that he was going into the river to find the crocodile. I protested. He insisted.

I could do nothing to dissuade him from going in or from being convinced that his "powerful" bracelets wouldn't shut the mouth of the crocodile if it was still alive. He slid down the steep embankment and stepped into the river, probing the water ahead of him with the long spear he always carried when we went hunting. It would be of little value against an attacking crocodile in that murky water. He was soon up to his neck and then swimming, always probing with his spear. Needless to say, I was praying for his safety. I couldn't remember ever being so uptight while flying. The search went on for a number of minutes. I kept suggesting that he give it up, giving all sorts of valid and invalid reasons. He finally emerged safely. He stood on the shore below, looking at the quiet water in frustration, and then came up the bank and sat down beside me. We talked quietly and watched. I thanked him for getting out of the river. I thanked God for getting him out safely. About five minutes passed when the eyes and nostrils of the unscathed crocodile slowly emerged from below the surface of the water a short distance from where Manja had just been.

The large reptile saw us and immediately submerged. It didn't appear again.

Manja was convinced of the spiritual power of his bracelets. I was convinced that his safety was the result of the grace of God, and told him so. We talked about it as we left the overhanging trees at the river's edge to go back to the village some five miles upstream. He was receptive but not convinced. That was going to take a special work of the Spirit of God. Over a period of months and through a series of personal contacts with Nigerian Christians and missionaries, Manja came to Christ. After several months of preparation he was baptized. It was a marvelous event. There is nothing more thrilling than to see a life committed to Christ. Several more years passed, and Manja grew in faith.

To prevent dependence on white missionaries we were going to Tissa much less on Sundays. I had not been there for several months. When I arrived one Sunday morning, I was told that Manja was ill. I asked to see him and was told he wasn't in the village. He had been taken away to a medicine man along the Takum-Yola road. I didn't like the sound of that, but didn't think it best to press the matter. Two of the older men said they would take me to him after the service.

We made our way back along the two-track and over the two precarious "bridges" to get back to the main road. We traveled over its rough, red, dusty surface for about two miles. Then they told me to stop at the next compound on the right. We got out of the pickup truck and walked up a gradual slope about a hundred yards along a narrow path in the tall grass to three shaggy-looking huts in an isolated compound.

Omaru, the older of the two men, announced our presence with his "Salama" (peace). There was no reply. We continued into the compound. The three grass-roofed huts were about ten feet apart in a semicircle. The low entrances faced the center. Their grass roofs were disheveled with age, rain, and winds. The walls had seen their share of rain coming through the roofs and looked as though some of their cracked and sunken mud bricks would come down completely in the next wet season. Broken cooking pots cluttered the unswept sand surface around the huts.

A mangy sand-colored dog let out a howl as our passing woke him from his late morning nap. He got up and skulked away behind the hut with his tail between his legs. Then there was just us, the hot sun, and the heavy silence in the dingy compound.

Omaru muttered something as we approached the low hut entrance where he and Tani knew Manja should be. Tani grunted in reply. Omaru bent over, repeated his "Salama," and entered. I followed him and Tani came in behind me. Our eyes had to adjust from the blazing light outside to the semidarkness of the hut. A sour odor permeated the air. Pots filled with leaves and liquids were spread in disarray along the far side of the hut. To the right lay Manja, silent and still. Tani spoke to him. There was no reply. Tani's voice reflected increased concern as he repeated, "Manja!" At the same time he stooped and put his hand on Manja's shoulder. Manja slowly rolled from his side to his back, opened his eyes, and indicated recognition. He was a desperately sick man. His speech was normally choppy and clipped. Now it was almost inaudible and painfully slow. He needed to muster a great deal of the little strength he had to speak at all. He stared through us as he struggled to say a few words. Then his eyes slowly closed.

I laid my hand on his forehead. He was feverish. I continued to try to make sense of it all. Why was he *here?*

As I pondered this, squatting next to Manja, we heard the shuffle of feet outside, then fumbling at the entrance. The form of a small, aged man entered. The medicine man treating Manja had returned. He greeted us in his cracked gravelly voice. Tani began to introduce me to him. I stood up with my eyes still fixed on Manja and then turned to him. I took his shriveled, bony hand, which had been mechanically extended, into mine. I looked into his wrinkled, sunken face. My eyes glanced into his. I suddenly felt overwhelmed by this whole affair. He was totally blind! I felt the situation was completely untenable! A Christian had been put into the hands of a blind medicine man in a filthy hut littered with pots full of local medical concoctions, some of which were undoubtedly lethal. I stood in the semidark hut with Omaru and Tani, whose intent I could not question, with one medicine man whose intent I could question, and in an environment that reeked with ignorance and possible wrongdoing. The victim lay helpless on a mat on the dirt floor.

As a white man there was little likelihood that I was going to find out all the elements that had put this grim business together. I felt what seemed to be an evil presence. Something had to be done. This couldn't go on. If I was going to get him out of here it would have to be with the consent of Omaru and Tani who were standing there with me. Thoughts raced through my mind, some angry, and some suspicious of the feared pagan elements in Tissa. I had to temper those thoughts with an overriding concern for Manja and the future of the whole witness and ministry to these people.

Excusing myself, I went outside to think and pray.

Calling for Omaru and Tani, I told them we had to think very seriously about this as Manja was close to death as far as I could tell. I told them bluntly that if he died here, without looking at other options for help, we would be responsible for his death. We spoke about taking him to the hospital. I said I could not make that decision, but needed their counsel. The discussion led to my driving to Takum twenty-five miles away to consult and possibly bring a doctor from the mission hospital back with me to assess Manja's condition. The doctor's advice was to go back and get Manja if possible.

When I returned to the hut, Omaru and Tani agreed that Manja be taken to the hospital. The medicine man was nowhere to be seen, so I didn't even ask about him. We carefully put Manja into the car I had substituted for the pickup truck. It took well over an hour to get him to the hospital. His condition appeared to be about the same when we arrived.

With each passing day there seemed to be some improvement. The doctors at the hospital were afraid he had been given medication which had damaged the liver. We prayed for him daily and hoped that treatment would be successful. We also hoped that no local medication would find its way into his system in addition to the treatment he was receiving at the hospital.

On one occasion, when I came to visit him, he was actually sitting up in his hospital bed. I was elated about the prospect of seeing him return to Tissa in health. We thanked God for his progress. A few days later, however, his progress stopped, things turned around, and once again his condition erroded day after day.

I was going to be gone for several days on a series of flights, so I went to the hospital at 6 A.M., an hour before flight time. His bed was empty. Neither his wife nor anyone else was around. I found the nurse on night duty. In response to my question he said,

"I am sorry, Suh. He died yesterday evening about 10 o'clock." He had been buried during the night. His relatives had gone into Takum town. I had no idea where they might be.

My heart was heavy as I rode down the hospital road to the airstrip. Only eternity would resolve all the unknowns about his sickness, his being brought to a pagan medicine man, his physical ups and downs in the hospital that defied diagnosis, and his death. I was sure he was a Christian, and so very thankful that of all those who were part of Tissa's middle and older age group, the one who had died was a Christian. Manja had come out of the depths of pagan practice. He had found faith in Christ before his numbered days on earth were finished. The gospel, which had been brought to Tissa and rejected long before Harold, Daniel, and I went there, has continued to make inroads. Because God is patient, and because He perseveres, there is bright hope for the future.

# 11

# Transatlantic in a
# Twin Comanche

The flight began, in some ways, long before the wheels left the runway at 7:22 A.M. on the 28th of July, 1972. Flight planning, charts, clearances, survival kit, spare parts, and other things all started coming together long before the trip. There were additional items such as the long-range tanks, Export Certificate of Airworthiness, and final inspection; and then the final loading. In spite of trying to plan and work ahead, details piled up during the last couple of days and pressures built. The clock did not stop, however. It brought me to that final preset date and time right on schedule.

A number of people came to the airport at Grand Rapids, Michigan. I had to say good-by to some very good friends and colleagues. The more difficult thing was saying good-by to my family. It would be different this time because I wouldn't be seeing them for a number of months. Anne was going to stay in the U.S. with our children; Jim was to begin college and Jaclynn was in her last year of high school. Two representatives from the Christian Reformed Board of World Mission offered prayer. I thanked those present for coming (I did appreciate it), but I was getting choked up about my family. I was very uncomfortable and rather hastily said my good-bys. I got hold of myself as I walked to the airplane parked on the ramp.

I climbed into the Twin Comanche over the monumental "lunch" my wife had prepared. It was in a cardboard box on the right front seat. That box was topped with charts, plotter, computer, and the flight plan sheets, filled with the information I had put on them during hours of planning. I called ground control after start up and told them I had filed an instrument flight plan to Gander, Newfoundland and requested my clearance. There was silence ... I am sure it was because of the length of the flight in the small plane. When the response came, I was told they had no flight plan on me. That was annoying because I had given additional advance notice per their request. They were very nice about it, however, and after giving them the information the second time, they came back with a clearance to Gander. I had done the runup and pre-takeoff check by this time. The tower cleared me for takeoff.

The airplane was heavy with the added fuel (one hundred extra gallons in tanks in the cabin), and the other parts and supplies I had on board for the trip. The Twin Comanche got off the ground well, but wasn't the stable airplane I was accustomed to, especially around the pitch axis. I was cleared over Lansing, Michigan, and then to Flint. It was a beautiful morning. The airplane climbed slowly, being overweight (legally so on a ferry permit). I had requested and was cleared to 11,000 feet. After being asked by Chicago and then Cleveland center about my rate of climb three times, I told them I was doing what I could, but had a lot of weight to contend with. About twenty miles east of Lansing I reached 11,000 feet and leveled off. The winds aloft forecast was favorable, and I started to make good time. The cloud below was scattered until Flint and then it was clear for some time. I passed over the southern corner of Lake Huron and on to London, Ontario. After St. Jean in Quebec, clouds began to appear below, and the tops got higher. I requested the Millinocket and Moncton weather. It was raining at both places, but there were no thunderstorms. Cloud tops reached my altitude so I requested 12,000 and then 13,000 feet. When that altitude didn't keep me on top I requested 14,000 feet, and I was thankful for the oxygen system. Ahead was an area that looked like dissipated weather. I decided to penetrate, rather than go around it. The ice was negligible. The radar showed no imbedded weather ahead. Fifty miles farther on I burst into sunshine with cloud tops varying from 14,000 feet down to an estimated 10,000 feet. I waited for about fifteen minutes to observe the trend in the cloud formations, and then requested descent to 13,000 feet. A little later it became evident that I was beyond any cloud that was going to be that high, so I asked for and was cleared to 11,000 feet. I stowed the oxygen mask and shut the oxygen off. The clouds below began breaking up rapidly. I requested 9,000 feet so that I could see more of the desolate rocky terrain and water below me. The little plane droned on hour after hour. My fuel reserve was good as I had been making great time. A groundspeed check later in the flight, however, indicated that I had slowed down considerably. That had been predicted in the winds aloft forecast so I wasn't concerned. I finally passed on to the island of Newfoundland. Center turned me over to Gander approach. After seven hours of nonstop flight it was nice to be in contact with the destination airport and know that the weather was good. I had not been in Gander before during daylight. The last time I was there was on a cutting, cold night in January, 1967, when ferrying a Piper Aztec to Nigeria. Now temperatures were in the high forties, which was warm by comparison.

I was grateful as the plane touched down after the long flight. I taxied to the international terminal and was through with customs and fueling in an hour. After checking over the airplane and eating supper, I went to the weather office to get a preliminary forecast for the route to Santa Maria in the Azore Islands, which was the next stop.

The report was mixed. It wasn't dangerous, but it wasn't going to be without problems either. There was a front near Delta, which was a ship based in the mid-Atlantic for air navigation and weather observation purposes. Winds were to be adverse initially. Then crosswinds from the southwest would neither hinder nor help me. After reaching the first of the Azore islands, I was to get a little help from the winds, but only five to ten knots. The front was not supposed to contain an abundance of heavy weather, but there were some thunderstorms in it. It was too widespread to even think of going around it.

I went to the hotel, called home, again thanked God for a good beginning, and went to bed. At 4:30 A.M. the alarm jarred me back to consciousness. I must have slept very well.

Shuffling over to the hotel window, I peered out. Lights in the dark street were visible for only a few hundred feet.

Thick ground fog obscured everything but the lights. A slow taxi trip to the airport disclosed only more of the same. I trotted upstairs to the weather office in the terminal building. The official weather was "sky obscured and visibility zero," but they were optimistic about it improving quite soon. After an hour it did pick up to a 100-foot ceiling and one-fourth mile visibility. My difficulty was that on takeoff, if I were to lose one engine with all that weight, the only way to go was down. I wouldn't be able to see the ground until I was virtually on it. Even the 100-foot ceiling they were giving was a part-time affair. Departing would have been possible, but hardly wise.

After breakfast and another briefing for the weather on my route to the Azores (consistent with what I had been told the day before), I went to the airplane to inspect it. I waited, reviewed my flight planning, and drank more tea. Two hours later weather was the same. Then it began to dramatically improve. I could discern a definite ceiling and see the large hangars across the field. The weather was now marginal but acceptable. I asked ground control for a confirmation on the exact runway heading so that I could make one last check on the compasses, which would be so very important, especially on this flight over the ocean. After taxiing to the end of runway fourteen I did the compass check, the takeoff check, and told them I was ready to copy clearance. I really appreciated that they had held my clearance for me over this long period. It was a lengthy clearance including all the reporting point coordinates (latitude and longitude) on the transatlantic flight.

Technically this takeoff was no different, and yet there were some things that separated it from others. The destination was a small island close to 2,000 miles away in a vast ocean. Most of the time during the flight would be spent spanning that ocean with nothing but seemingly endless water below. There would be none of the normal landmarks or radio beacons available. The first time I flew across the ocean I knew that academically, but now I was anticipating what I had already experienced. The challenge was exciting, but the known consequences of error or malfunction of vital equipment, evoked subtle, but not unnoticed, apprehension deep inside. To be totally without apprehension seemed to me to be either ignorant or foolhardy. Apprehension did not alter my commitment, but there was a distinctly accelerated surge of mental activity and calculation in the otherwise rather mechanical action of pushing the throttles to takeoff power as the small plane began to move down the runway.

With the temperature at forty-one degrees Fahrenheit, the airplane responded well. It accelerated rapidly and briskly rose from the runway. After climbing a few hundred feet, I was enveloped in the low cloud. A few minutes later I broke out of the top of the layer into the brilliant sunshine above and the endless expanse of the bright, white cloud deck below. I climbed higher and higher above it, knowing it was going to be a long time before the next stop.

Headwinds to St. John weren't very encouraging, and I was hoping the weather briefers were right about the wind switch once out to sea. After passing the coast of Newfoundland at 11,000 feet the cloud deck below began to break up. The ocean became visible and very impressive. The waves on its massive surface glittered in the sun.

I tracked outbound on the St. John nondirectional beacon to the next reporting point, Tarpon intersection, which is 111 nautical miles to the southeast. After calculating that I had arrived at Tarpon, I made the turn to the east-southeast and reported my position to Gander radio. I put in the heading correction computed from the winds aloft forecast and the little Twin Comanche purred on. I ate a couple of apples as time went on. The weather was beautiful. The sky was clear above and the vast blue sea undulated in swells below.

I wrote down the time over Tarpon and then estimated the time to the next reporting point, which was just a latitude and longitude coordinate. The next reporting point of any verifiable significance would be over ship Delta. There were several hundred miles during which time I had to fly only a compass heading, but ship Delta would eventually be within range of the standard navigation equipment on board. I cruised on at 11,000 feet with a feeling of confidence and trust, but also with the definite sense of minuteness that this kind of environment produces.

My appetite on such flights is very limited. I am a better gobbler than a nibbler when it comes to food anyway, so puttering around with it to kill time has no appeal. I would eat something periodically, check times and distances, watch gauges and headings, monitor the radio, and make the occasional required position report using the long distance, high-frequency radio equipment on board. Out of curiosity, I looked for ships, but saw none. I was not flying along the shipping lanes. If I had seen one I might have had more reason to think I was lost than reason to be delighted in finding a ship out there. There were times when I just sat and soaked in the vastness of it all.

Then the inevitable front began to appear. Several hundred miles off in the distance there was that yellow-white area between the sea and the blue sky. As time passed it became more definitive. The front was there as they said it would be, and it was hundreds of miles long. Gradually more cloud appeared below and some at my altitude. Outside air temperature was eight degrees Centigrade and slowly going up, so there was no ice problem in the offing. Cumulus cloud became mixed with the stratus. I was approaching the frontal system from the rear. The weather radar began to show small cells which I went around, but cloud was getting thicker and darker. Gander radio had asked me if I wanted Delta's equipment turned on an hour before my estimated time for passage over Delta and an hour afterward. I confirmed that. I was now getting a non-directional beacon signal from the ship which was reassuring even though it indicated I was slightly north of course. I tried to raise them on the VHF radio, but couldn't. A jet aircraft was coming in the opposite direction at 33,000 feet. I asked the pilot what the weather looked like from his perspective. He said he thought I could pick my way through the stuff. I smiled a little, thinking, "This gentleman speaks from a position of strength with his altitude and equipment." He was soon many miles to the northwest. At least I was by myself in a lot of sky, so deviations for weather would be no problem. Gander radio's question about ship Delta's equipment being turned on only for my sake confirmed that. The radar didn't show any hard-core cells, but it was indicating some real paint-stripping rain. I didn't care to investigate the degree of turbulence, and neither did I care to arrive in Nigeria with an airplane that needed a paint job on the wing's leading edges, so I stayed out of the heavy rain as much as possible. My radio contact with Gander and New York had been good, but getting clearance for every deviation in this accumulating weather mass was impossible, so I tried Delta on VHF again. They responded, and I simply kept them informed of what I was doing about altitude and headings. They picked me up on radar. That was also reassuring. I had to take up a heading of about ninety degrees magnetic for a while due to weather. That was a general direction about which I meandered rather generously. I was getting quite far north of course, but I didn't want to get into the heavier weather. The heavy rain, which had become unavoidable, would subside a bit and then start all over. Thankfully there was no lightning or significant turbulence. I was on instruments, keeping out of areas that I didn't like the looks of on the radar scope, while trying to stay as far south as possible. Without radar I would have thrown in the towel at this point because visual appearance would have convinced anyone that there was nothing else to do. I continued to pick my way through the massive gray front. Once again I was deeply impressed with my own insignificant size. Rain streamed off the windshield. Time and miles sped by.

I was almost due north of Delta. Suddenly I burst into sunshine and beautiful blue sky. The wall of gray with its abundant rain and threat of something worse was behind me. I turned to a heading of almost due south, but strong winds out of the southwest soon squashed any ideas of passing directly over Delta without taking up a south-southwest heading. I was not about to do that. I was getting position checks from Delta often enough to be sure (by correlating my heading and speed) that what he saw on his scope was in fact the airplane I was flying. Additionally there was nobody else out there to see. I reported to New York when I was abeam Delta.

Now that I was out of the weather I could check the fuel in the ferry tanks again. I did this with an ordinary carpenter's rule, converting inches to gallons. It was not very difficult. I only had to multiply by two. Having done that, I recalculated my fuel endurance. It was satisfactory.

It was good to be beyond the weather. But my southerly progress and ground speed reported by Delta was of some concern.

The winds were much stronger than forecast, and I had a long way to go to the Azores. I asked Delta to let me know when I was on their 123 degree radial. This would put me back on course after my long detour to the north to get through the front. Delta offered to send up a balloon for a winds aloft report, if I wanted it. Should I refuse that sort of service? Never. I thanked him and a short time he came back reporting a 47-mile-an-hour wind rather than the 15-mile-an-hour wind which was forecast. I corrected for it and was soon slightly south of my course. I reasoned that Delta was right at the edge of the front. They were probably getting much stronger upper winds there than I was, being out ahead of the front. I again adjusted my headings, but it was necessarily a bit of guess work. Delta and I had a little pleasant talk, and I explained the purpose for the flight and the airplane. After a bit we said good-by.

About two hours later I tuned in the Horta NDB (non-directional beacon). Horta is the most westerly island of the Azores. I was still several hundred miles out, but found the signal to be coming in much stronger than I had expected. That was great, and I found I needed somewhat less correction to the south than I was using.

The sun was getting low in the west. Darkness would come long before I reached the Azores, but the weather was good as had been forecasted for this part of the flight.

The sun slowly sank into the sea behind me. The master of color stroked the sky with brilliant orange which changed to softer pinks. Then shades of scarlet became deep purples. The blue of the sea turned gray and then black. The sky and the sea finally blended in blackness while myriads of twinkling stars gave space and dimension to a breathtaking canopy. The ocean seemed larger, and the small plane even smaller.

The transatlantic flight of the Twin Comanche.

I was making my position reports, but knew that the one at "Mike," which is only a geographical reporting point twenty-five miles off Flores, would have to be rather accurate. A practical and most satisfying use of the radar was in the offing. When I thought it was time, I switched it on. After the warm-up period I turned it to the eighty-mile range. There was the island of Flores, a shape on the scope exactly thirty-eight miles away, straight on course, with a little island next to it also showing up on the scope. That was beautiful! I could make the positon report at Mike and give an estimate for Flores which would be accurate to the minute.

It was getting later, and I was feeling the effects of a long day. I estimated Santa Maria, my destination, at about 11:30 P.M. Lajes was the alternate and weather there was good. Santa Maria's weather was also good, but they did have some low cloud and conditions that could produce fog if the trend continued.

Three small lights on the island became visible in the darkness as I flew toward Horta. After passing Flores, the darkness returned, except for the stars. Later the reddish-orange edge of the moon slowly emerged on the horizon. At about the same time I saw a tiny light flash slightly to the left. It was a lighthouse on one of the islands. More lights appeared as time passed. The moon rose higher and changed to yellow and then to silver. It hung above the sea and islands like a huge ball with its upper right edge lopped off. It continued to rise directly ahead, reflecting on the restless water. The gray 7,600-foot peak at Horta rose out of the shimmering silver path in the sea.

San Miguel was coming up. It was the last island before landing. I was happy to be able to call Santa Maria approach when passing the last reporting point. I gave them an estimate of only eighteen minutes later (11:33 P.M.) for Santa Maria. I was cleared to descend. At 4000 feet I could see the airport, so I requested a visual approach and a "straight in" for the long north-south runway. After reporting the airport "in sight," I told the tower I was glad to see it in an ad-lib fashion. He asked me to "say again." I did, but his ability in English (he was Portuguese) and this unnecessary chatter didn't get along well. After another request to say it again I told him to, "disregard." He got that, and I got rid of my informality.

I felt I had to be very careful, due to fatigue, so I tuned in the ILS (instrument landing system) and followed the glide slope. I checked to be sure the landing gear was down about four times and did the rest of the necessary prelanding checks. I touched down, taxied to the terminal, went through customs and immigration formalities, and even had a midnight supper. The Lord had been very good and I thanked Him.

I went to the hotel. The gentleman on night duty at the hotel discouraged me from trying to make a telephone call to my wife and kids that night. His reasons didn't sound very objective to me, but I didn't have a great deal of push left to argue the point, and Anne was not necessarily expecting to hear that night anyway. I had been busy for twenty hours and felt like it. I collapsed into the aged, sagging bed in the rather dingy room, but it felt like something out of a Hilton.

I got a call through to Anne the next day, which I spent relaxing on the ground. I had scheduled this break before the next two days of flight.

I hired one of the few taxis available and toured the island. The narrow roads wound through lush green pastures. Quaint little white homes dotted the landscape. Small farms were bordered by rock terraces and low, thick rock walls. A few head of cattle grazed quietly on the hills. People worked in the fields. A farmer walked behind a plow drawn by a single ox. It was quiet and serene; a good place to rest. A Roman Catholic church stood tall in the main town. The people living on the island were almost all Catholic. I stood on the top of the highest hill. From there I could see almost the entire island, and I wondered how many of its ten thousand inhabitants really knew the God who had placed them in this semitropical grandeur so far out in the ocean. The sea folded its gentle swells over the rocks which studded the shoreline below the cliffs. These cliffs formed a barrier from the sea for much of the island. At some places steep slopes flared and met the rolling surf with dark gray beaches. The lower regions of those slopes were patched with grape vineyards. I looked to the south where the island plunged into the sea over a rocky cliff. My eyes reached out and beyond, to where the sky met the ocean. All being well, that was where tomorrow would take me.

After some delay in getting a taxi at 4:30 the next morning, I finally arrived at the airport. I paid all my bills. It cost more to keep the airplane there than it did to keep me there, even with my call to the States. With spiritual and physical preparations complete, I was ready to be on the way to Dakar, Senegal, sixteen hundred miles away. I received my long clearance and taxied out.

All the external and the two additional cabin fuel tanks were full again. The response to the application of full power on takeoff was less than spirited because of the added weight. I slowly gained momentum down the runway toward the edge of the cliff. The air was warm and humid. The breeze was light. At eighty knots I put back pressure on the control yoke, and the tiny twin rose from the runway.

I tucked the landing gear away as soon as I was sure the plane was going to stay in the air. The end of the runway passed beneath. Moments later the surface dropped vertically into the ocean. Waves plowed into the rocky base of the cliff and hurled their energy into the air. At 1,400 feet I slipped into the overcast. A monotonous gray surrounded the plane until several thousand feet higher. The gray turned to silver above, then to a bright white, and suddenly sunlight flooded the cabin. A canopy of clear blue above was complemented by a carpet of snowy white below, as I broke out of the top of the thick, stratus cloud deck. The heavy little plane labored to 11,000 feet and leveled off.

The cloud deck below began to have lower tops, dropping farther and farther below the airplane. Then areas of glistening sea became visible. The broken cloud below became scattered and then disappeared altogether. The sea was placid, and the air was smooth. The tailwind forecast was accurate. I was making excellent speed and getting nearer to the African continent by the hour. Radio communcations, however, were difficult. I was finally able to contact the Canary Islands and later Dakar, my destination.

I saw the first ship making its way to the African coast. As I began to almost parallel the west coast of Africa, more ships appeared. I was beginning to get solid readings on the navigation instruments. That, combined with the number of hours I had been in the air, all indicated that I would soon see the shore of the African continent. The trip was beautiful. There was no significant weather. I gained almost an hour due to tail winds and arrived in Dakar at 5:25 P.M. local time.

After going through all the formalities at the airport, a friendly Air Afrique Airline employee managed to find a hotel room for me. I arrived at the modern multi-story hotel, situated on a small bay, only to find out that I had been placed in one of the rooms in the annex. That was no problem — I thought. The "annex," however, turned out to be a number of individual huts in the back lot. That was not bad either, except that the air conditioner in the one I was to occupy was not operating, and there were no other rooms available. I walked into the large hut. It was like a furnace inside. It had double shutters on opposite walls which could be opened. I decided I would do just that and enjoy the sound of the waves lapping on the beach during the night. I became concerned about the mosquito population, however, when I opened the shutters and found no screens covering the openings. I opened them just long enough to let some fresh air in the round room. The breeze from the nearby sea quickly cooled it down.

I went to the dining room for supper and got a phone call through to Anne. I decided to go to bed early and returned to the hut. Thankfully I found the right one in the dark. I took a shower, had devotions (thanking God especially for getting me to the African continent), and laid down to — well, as I soon realized — sweat. The room had regained most of its heat because its very warm walls and grass roof had baked in the sun all day. It was unpleasant, but I thought, "You will just have to forget it, my friend, and go to sleep. You have a big day tomorrow." Then I heard the first whining flight of a mosquito. It was getting closer, so I knew he was up to no good. Now there is nothing in the world that will keep me awake like a mosquito when I have no mosquito net. I have something against sharing my blood supply with them. I was lying on the bed clothed in just my shorts. Even a sheet was unthinkable in the heat. This one, and any others which might have gained entrance, had a lot to bite besides my head. They bit and bit. I sweated and drearily swatted and then started to scratch places where mosquitoes were or had been. Opening the windows would cool me off, but also invite in numberless other mosquito visitors. I decided to open the windows and ask for a spray can to kill the mosquitoes. I had earlier heard an Englishman asking for a spray can, so I knew they had such things.

I went to the office and made my request — and waited. I asked again — and waited. It was getting near to 11:00 P.M. The steward finally came and gave me a spray can. I returned to the room, shut the shutters, and sprayed the place. Then I laid down to croak in the spray. It wasn't as bad as I thought. Soon I heard a mosquito and was slightly discouraged. Apparently, however, he was in a semicontrolled descent on his way to oblivion because neither that one nor any other bothered me again. The place had cooled down somewhat, and with the help of the spray I slipped into unconsciousness or fell asleep. (Seriously, I sprayed moderately.)

For some reason I woke up at 4:10 A.M. I thought I might as well get moving and committed the day to the Lord. Dakar weather was fine, while the enroute forecast from Conakry, Guinea, to Monrovia, Liberia, looked problematic but not prohibitive. I really had no idea of how accurate the forecast might or might not be. I started the engines at 5:10. I had filed for 6:00 A.M. departure, but it was no problem to them if I left earlier. I had chosen to go around the coast and stay out to sea rather than cross over all the countries on the way to Lagos, since this avoided having to get all the over-flight clearances involved. I was off at 5:22 with a clearance that really didn't clear me anywhere but to 5000 feet. I wasn't worried about the clearance as we could straighten that out once airborne. Air traffic control had my flight plan, and they accepted my estimates after lifting off the runway. I made a long turn back to the south to get on course.

The airplane was heavy and sluggish in the warm air. The lights of Dakar passed under and behind me. The few lights along the coast faded as I traveled south and farther out to sea. My first reporting point was one hundred miles south. At that point I would take up a new heading that would take me roughly parallel to the coast. The sky changed from black to gray in the east. Visibility was good. I could see occasional flashes of lightning far in the distance, indicating that the weather they had predicted was there and active. I had not eaten any breakfast so I opened a can of chocolate drink that my wife had put in the "lunch" four days ago. I ate a few apples and continued to cruise in the smooth air as darkness changed to daylight. Low and medium cloud began to increase with some cumulus scattered through it. The radar began to paint strong cells.

The next few hours were hectic. Communications in precipitation were bad. To get a clearance amended for altitude or heading can be a time-consuming proposition. I monitored center, towers, and approaches as I passed significant airports, and did what was necessary to keep out of thunderstorms. About noon, I finally reached the edge of the weather, far to the east of where it was forecast to terminate. There was a stratus deck with small cumulus puffs breaking its flat top. The fatiguing, weather-dodging ordeal made me less than enthusiastic about the long sit I had ahead of me before arriving in Lagos, but it was a relief to be able to hold course, communicate, and catch up on paperwork. My fuel situation was no problem. The weather ahead was good. Being thankful for the blessing of progress, I passed Accra and then Contonou. The coast came into sight. I was skimming over the top of a cloud layer that had some breaks in it, approaching Lagos. I was cleared to 3500 feet and picked up the airport visually about five miles out through a break in the cloud. I requested a visual approach, which was approved, and touched down eleven hours and ten minutes after I had left Dakar. I thanked God that we had this new piece of equipment safely in Nigeria and could now put it to work in His service. Many phone calls and telegrams during the next several days were necessary to get the aircraft deregistered in the United States and registered in Nigeria. Because of this lengthy process, it wasn't until the following Monday that I was able to go on to Takum.

At five that afternoon I landed and taxied up to the Takum hangar where a group of missionaries and Nigerians were waiting. After I had greeted all of them, Rev. Les Van Essen, the mission's General Secretary, led in a dedication service of the airplane. It was an appropriate beginning.

I lay in bed that night contemplating the past days. I smiled when I thought of the tense moments in heavy weather. I felt contentment when I thought of the beauty of God's earth and sky. I was happy and grateful when I thought of God's goodness through it all. I thought of Anne and our children, Jim and Jacie, and felt uneasy with separation from them. My mind raced through the whole psychological and spiritual process which had brought us, as a family, to this point. I took comfort and courage and trusted.

The sound of African crickets and the distant rumble of thunder faded as I slipped into sleep.

# 12

# Flying the Dead and the Dying

Medical emergency flights had a basic similarity, yet each was different. They usually began rather abruptly, often coming by way of a note from the hand of an anxious-looking person who had been traveling by truck, motorcycle, or bicycle for a number of hours, or by being interjected over the mission radio, taking precedence over all other messages. The last few weeks had brought more than the average number, three in four days from one station.

Each medical flight was both a problem and an opportunity. On one flight the young lady died halfway back to Takum. On another the lady would, according to the medical people at Takum Christian Hospital, have died within a few hours had we not been able to get her. On another we received word too late to make the flight that day. All night the woman involved lay at Serti with a broken arm and a broken hip and other cuts and bruises. She had jumped in terror with her baby in her arms from a fast-moving passenger truck as the driver careened wildly over the dirt road. She received all the help she could get at Serti but had to wait until morning to get to the hospital. Lack of any navigation aids or ground lighting at the airstrips prevented night landings. I disturbed the early morning quiet by taking off before it was light, set a course for Serti, and waited for darkness to pass. I did this only when it was medically warranted, and then in a twin engine airplane, landing after daylight. The baby died, but the woman regained consciousness during the night and recovered after being flown to the hospital.

One never knows what the results of these flights will be. Problems occurred while coming back from Serti where I had picked up a beautiful, but very sick child about five years old, who was being held by her mother and anxiously observed by her father. We had to come through some weather. The tossing about of the small plane was disconcerting, especially to my passengers, as it was all new. It was also disconcerting to me because I knew it added discomfort and fear to already anxious parents. The little girl lay limp in her mother's arms. We stayed below the gray ragged cloud bases, but stormy winds whipped over the hills and the airplane behaved accordingly. The mother began to cry shortly after we had passed through the weather. Initially I thought it was fear. Communication between us was bad. They were from the Tiv tribe and didn't speak English or Hausa. I spoke virtually no Tiv. The father, however, indicated that the child was the reason for the tears. I felt the child's pulse. Her black eyes stared into space. There was no reaction, but she was breathing and I could feel a weak pulse. We had fifteen minutes of a thirty-five minute flight left. Anne often stood by on the radio at home, and I had reason to believe that there were medical people from Takum Hospital at Lupwe, just a few miles from the Takum airstrip. I transmitted "blind" and asked that she have them meet the plane at the strip. She couldn't acknowledge (no government approval for mission ground-to-air communications at that time), so I didn't know until we arrived whether or not the message was received. It was. The child was rushed to the hospital as soon as we taxied in. I was relieved and grateful to God for such splendid cooperation. We had done everything we could do.

But it doesn't always end well. The little child died that evening.

We didn't know that. When Anne and I went to check at the hospital the next morning, right after the church service, neither the child nor her parents were to be found. We will likely never see them again. In some cases all one can do is work and trust, hoping the brief encounter has been helpful, if not physically, then spiritually.

On one occasion I was asked to fly the corpse of the wife of a government teacher from India to Ganye, a remote town in northern Nigeria for burial. It was the only place in Nigeria this man had any acquaintances. They were other teachers from India who were stationed with him in Ganye. He, his wife, and his young daughter had come to Jos for the delivery of the second child. His wife and the infant died in childbirth. The Roman Catholic Mission made the request for the flight to Ganye. The young woman died in their hospital. They brought the corpse, wrapped in a white cloth, to the airport. We quietly placed it in the airplane. Two Catholic nuns, the husband, the little child, and I prayed together before we departed from Jos. The husband was a Hindu — a very disturbed man. His beautiful little two-and-a-half-year-old child dozed intermittently on his lap beside me during the long 260 miles in the airplane from Jos to Ganye. Her father looked forlornly out of the window.

We descended as we approached Ganye and flew low over the school at which he taught. The school was located seven miles south of the airstrip. We did so several times, but saw no visible response. We turned north to the airstrip and landed. There were no facilities at the Ganye airstrip, so when we got out of the plane, there was no place to go. Staying in it under the circumstances didn't seem appropriate either.

A Nigerian on a motorcycle saw the airplane land and rode over to us from the nearby dirt road. I explained what had happened. He graciously offered to get someone from the school.

We left the silent, shrouded form of the young mother's body in the privacy of the plane. The husband slowly walked over to a block of concrete used as an airplane tiedown and sat on it. He guided his little daughter between his raised knees. She leaned against him. He folded his arms around her. I walked over and sat on the ground a few feet away. Trying to comfort and witness to a grief-stricken Hindu Indian in the middle of nowhere is no easy task. Humanly speaking it is hopeless. I tried, as a Christian, to share in his sorrow.

We waited — and waited.

Time passed, and with it were going the remaining minutes of daylight. I could not make myself approach him about taking the corpse out of the airplane. There was no place to go with it, and he could not be left alone at a time like this. Planes don't often come into that strip so a large number of Nigerians, many of them children, were gathering. Word was passed, and they knew what had happened. Their behavior was considerate. We continued to wait.

It was about fifty minutes flying time back to Takum. The minutes slipped by, but no car came. The Takum option passed. It was twenty-five minutes to Serti. That was still possible.

I attempted sympathetic conversation with the burdened father, but he seemed to prefer silence. He was stunned and grief-stricken. During the periods of silence my mind was divided between the immediate concern with him and his daughter and my own commitments.

The pressure of the next day's flight schedule, the lack of communications between myself and Lupwe from this point, with the resultant concern it would cause, continually came to my mind. I suppressed any thoughts about leaving.

More time passed, and then a car with a heavyset Indian and his wife drove on to the dirt strip. I quietly greeted them and briefly explained. They knew nothing about the death due to lack of communication between Jos and this place. They recovered from the shock after a moment and then proceeded to walk over to the father, sitting with bowed head, his little daughter still between knees. Things came apart emotionally. It was the deep, but quiet crying of a man in grief. They walked him to the car. A dull, muffled, but sincere groan of sympathy ran through the crowd gathered around.

After a few minutes the heavyset Indian came over to me to ask about the corpse. We agreed to transfer it to the car, which was done without any difficulty.

Then there was nothing more I could do. They said I should go. I asked him to move the car some distance away so I wouldn't blow dust all over everybody when I started up. I bade the father good-by as best I could under the circumstances, climbed in the airplane, started up, and taxied away. The car drove slowly around the large group of people and down the dirt road, disappearing in the dust.

A few minutes later I was airborne and climbing past the steep mountain walls near Ganye. With time, daylight, and distance being what it was, I had to force myself to forget the situation I had just come out of and make some decisions. I climbed to 5500 feet hoping to get a little help from the winds on the way to Serti. Weather didn't help. The radar painted a line of thunderstorms just east of course and paralleling it. Serti was the destination and Baissa the alternate, which I could still make in daylight. If that failed I would go to Jos and land with flares, or to Kano which is 325 miles away and has lights. I had adequate fuel on board.

The little Twin Comanche passed over and sometimes between the mountain peaks ahead of the thunderstorms. The ominous dull gray to the east was broken by stabbing strokes of repeated lightning. About fifteen miles out of Serti it became certain that I could get in. The weather had not reached Serti and wouldn't before I got there. I landed and rolled up to the station which is right at the end of the strip.

Abe Vreeke, who was posted at Serti, rushed to the plane wondering about the reason for this unscheduled landing. I related the sad event from which I had just come.

Darkness, no plane arrival, and a set policy as to what to do about that, brought Anne to the radio at Lupwe at 6:30 P.M. I responded from Serti and again was reminded of what a terrific blessing the station-to-station radios were.

Little did I know that I had invited myself to Abe's birthday dinner, and I ate with the happy family that night. What a contrast to the situation which I had left so shortly before.

After the diesel generator, which lights the station until 10:00 P.M. gasped through its last noisy revolution, I was conscious of the quiet of the African night. I thought of the Hindu who would bury his young wife in the morning. I thought of his undefined and emotional verbal response to my questions and attempts to communicate with him in his grief. He could only say "There is belief." I felt pity for him and was disturbed by my own inadequacy in the situation. At the same time I gave praise to God for the clarity, the objectivity, the well-founded faith I had in Him, through Christ. And I couldn't help but evaluate a little. Do we appreciate it and articulate it enough?

# Dangerous Diversion*

One of the delights of being in Africa was the anticipation of an annual vacation with family and friends. We often spent it in the remote areas of northern Cameroon. Anne and I enjoyed our work, but we also looked forward to getting away from the radio messages, flight requests, pressures of flying, correspondence, and all the other things that made up "normal" living. We could also be with our children which was a very special occasion. We camped in some of the best of the African bush. We all enjoyed it. It was physical and mental refreshment because of the change. It was spiritually stimulating, with time to think, read, and fellowship. It was usually uninterrupted fun. We caught fish out of the rivers, kept ourselves in fresh meat by hunting, and shared great amounts of it with the Cameroonians with whom we hunted. We also shared the gospel with them.

We had lived in Nigeria for thirteen years, and I had a reasonable amount of experience in hunting everything from goat-sized duikers to buffaloes and elephants. Being a missionary pilot, I had also transported patients who had been gored by buffaloes, mauled by leopards, or torn badly by crocodile jaws. I had visited with these people in our hospitals and was well aware of the dire consequences of making mistakes when hunting dangerous animals.

Some of the animals we hunted were dangerous. Everything had always gone well until one nearly fatal incident.

We had gone to Cameroon as a family along with missionary

*This material used in edited form with permission of *Outdoor Life* Magazine, who originally published the story in January 1972.

friends. We camped in tents along the Rey River. My son Jim had been hunting with me but didn't feel well that particular morning, so I hunted by myself with two Cameroonian trackers. We had walked several miles seeing and passing up some mediocre hartebeest. A warthog scooted into the thicket when we disturbed him, but I was more interested in getting a buffalo. Much of the bush was rather open savanna, but we came across and then entered an area of tall trees. The high foliage was thick but did not completely shut out the sunlight. As we walked through the sunspeckled undergrowth I noticed that it had been tramped down by various animals. Indications were that the area had been visited by elephants. We could walk very quietly among the tall trees and through the undergrowth as the elephants had crushed the fallen leaves to minute particles. One of the trackers, who was walking ahead of me, stopped and pointed to fresh buffalo tracks. We soon came on droppings. Almost immediately after that he again froze, squatted slowly, and, without even turning to see if I was looking, motioned me to come. I moved up to him quietly to see one buffalo after another appear through the foliage. They were about eighty yards away. The wind was slight and in our favor. There was enough cover to get a lot closer. I stalked to within thirty yards of the nearest animal. The scrubby undergrowth was thicker where they were feeding, but occasional grunts and movements indicated that there were a lot more buffaloes than I could distinctly see. The one I could see best was a cow. When she raised her head I'd freeze, then she would lower her head and resume feeding. I spent about ten minutes playing this tense game. Then the wind, as often happens about midmorning that time of year, became variable. I knew what was going to happen, and I quickly scanned the parts of buffaloes I could see, trying to pick out a good head.

Trying didn't help one bit. We heard a snort, and about twenty-five buffaloes piled out, pounding across and in front of us about forty yards away. I saw what I wanted, but passed it up because it is too dangerous to shoot a running buffalo unless it is already hit and one is trying to finish the job. We watched them go, impressed with their sheer brute force.

African trackers are never much impressed with that sort of thing. They much prefer meat on the ground to meat pounding off on the hoof. I received questioning glances and explained that I could not see a good bull in the undergrowth. The trackers knew

the wind switch had spooked them, so there were no further problems except what to do next. We decided to follow the buffaloes.

The herd went through several dry creek beds, over some higher
ground, and wound up in a dried-up swamp about a mile and a
half from where they had started. They were grazing out of the
high end of the swampy area when we saw them again. They were
moving away slowly, but doing a lot of looking behind as they
went. We could not stay completely concealed and still see what
we needed to see. They saw us and again bolted. David, the head
tracker, was familiar with the area. He said they would turn to
our left after going around a knoll which was quite heavily treed.
We dashed through the trees and undergrowth and over the knoll
to intercept them.

On reaching the far side we saw the buffaloes just as they were
breaking their run and walking into another wooded area about
two hundred yards across open lowland. They stopped momen-
tarily. We were close enough so that with a scope it wasn't a
difficult shot. I used a tree trunk as a rest, but I was panting after
all that running, and my heart was pounding. I saw a big brute
near the rear of the herd. I lined up on him, but I was very conscious of my rapid breathing and heart beat. They had escaped
twice and I was hurting to get this thing done. Just as I was set
to shoot, the herd started to move away at a slow walk. I swung
with the animal and squeezed off the shot. The buffalo lurched in
such a way that I knew he was hit, and I heard the familiar sound
of the bullet sock into the big frame. The herd disappeared in a
cloud of dust and entered a heavier section of growth. We followed. Finding blood was no problem. After about fifty yards the
wounded animal left the herd and stood still. About one hundred
fifty yards farther, the wounded buffalo heard us coming and got
underway. We only heard him; we couldn't see him because of the
large patch of unburnt, tall grass. There was a pool of blood on
the ground, however, where the animal had stood. A half-hour
later I got a fleeting glimpse of the buffalo as he tore off through
undergrowth and tall grass. An hour later we ran across a con-
centration of blood, but it wasn't the bright red lung blood I had
hoped for. Again we heard hoof beats and heavy rustling as the
animal moved off.

At about 1 P.M. we sat down alongside a dry riverbed to talk
things over. We were under a gigantic tree; it was a relief to be

out of the heat of the sun. Since no one else was hunting in the area, we decided to leave the sticky affair until the next morning, giving the buffalo a chance to stiffen up or die. We could also make arrangements to follow the dangerous, wounded animal with the advantage of having two armed people. We trudged back to the Landrover and drove to camp.

At camp it was decided that Roger Ingold would go along to finish the job. Roger, a native of Indiana, was the superintendent of the Church of the Brethren Mission in Nigeria, an able hunter who keeps his cool. We prayed together about what we knew could be a very dangerous business.

At 7 o'clock the next morning we were on the animal's trail again. At times we made good progress, but at other times it was painfully slow. I was amazed at the tracker's ability to pursue the buffalo without following anything more obvious than dislodged pebbles, cracked leaves, or other very minor surface disturbances. I felt like a third grader trying to keep up with a college professor. The African just kept at it, patiently and persistently, often showing me a sign that I couldn't see clearly let alone interpret.

We followed the tracks for about an hour and a half to where they ended at a stream. On the other side we picked them up again, but it was time for a break from the strain. We sat down under the tall trees, and it was only then that I became aware of the small pouches of food the trackers had brought along. This was unusual since they normally carried no food, but was a good indication that they were going to see this thing through. After a short time we set out again, walking in single file. The tracker went first. Behind him was the Cameroonian guide. I followed him. Roger was behind me and the two meat carriers walked behind him. They often dropped back thirty to fifty yards or more.

Blood had been very sparse and was dried almost black wherever we found it. Sometimes we would go a hundred yards or more before finding another drop of it, and then it would be no more than that. The fact that the buffalo was not continuing to lose blood of any significance disturbed us. Everything indicated that I had lit the fuse the day before. We were just waiting for the explosion of a buffalo charging out at us. In open areas we relaxed just a little, feeling that the charge wouldn't likely occur there, and if it did there would be more time to cope with it.

Sometimes it was a matter of gulping hard, knowing I couldn't allow a tracker to go into thickly foliaged areas, long grass, or spotty jungle without following right behind him. In order to do that I had switched places with the guide and followed the tracker closely. We went through what seemed to be a hundred places where the brute should have been, but there was nothing, except the prospect of a worse place ahead.

Suddenly a heavy crashing in the bush just ahead and to the right warned us that the beast was coming at us full tilt. A moment later the animal appeared. He was all too close and coming fast. To our left was tall grass. The tracker and the guide catapulted into it and disappeared instantly. The buffalo had first directed its charge at the tracker. With him gone, I was next in the small open area. The buffalo had charged in a direction across and in front of me. There was a tree about six inches in diameter about six feet from me. He was going to pass behind it and to the left. I quickly moved a step to the left to get in a shot, but the buffalo shifted direction in one bound and headed straight for me. He came for me to the right of the tree, which meant he would pass behind it. I put the sight of my .375 H & H Winchester Model 70 on his neck. I concentrated on placing the shot, so much so that I didn't anticipate his rapid passage behind the small tree, and got the shot off a split second too late. The bullet crashed into the edge of the tree as his neck passed behind it.

An instant later his massive head and horns slammed into my lower chest. I was thrown flat on my back, my hat, sunglasses, and rifle all going in various directions. What had happened took about three seconds, and Roger had no opportunity to shoot because of the direction from which the buffalo came. While the buffalo and I thrashed violently in a fury of flying grass and dust, Roger shot over its back in an effort to distract it. The huge head pulled as the shot boomed, and I rolled away as fast as I could. That gave Roger room to shoot the beast, and his rifle boomed again. In a flurry of motion I got up on my feet, facing the buffalo, but moving rapidly the other way when I saw him collapse. I had gained momentum and brushed past Roger, almost knocking him over. I stopped, still on my feet but a bit groggy, and thanked him profusely for saving my life. Roger put another 300-grain bullet from his .378 Weatherby into the neck of the fallen beast, and then he looked at me with some concern.

I became aware of a burning sensation in my chest. Roger and

I stopped and looked at it as we took a few paces together toward the buffalo. I had a deep gouge in my chest which was more of a hole than a tear and I was blood all over. My face had a long, superficial cut down one side. About a quarter of my camouflage hunting shirt had been torn away. I felt a little woozy and lay down. Roger knelt beside me and examined the hole in my chest. We were convinced from the way it looked, and by my breathing, that the horn had not penetrated my lungs. We gave thanks to God.

Just then the worried Cameroonian trackers and guide appeared. Roger started to clean out the wound. There was some chest hair stuck in the gouge so he took out his knife to cut it away. The Cameroonians were greatly concerned with my appearance and gave the impression that they thought I was about to die. When Roger took the knife out they must have thought he was going to finish the job out of kindness. They were horrified and put up an awful fuss. He explained his intention, and they were relieved as well as a little embarrassed.

Using toilet paper, pieces of my shirt, and some drinking water, Roger cleaned me up a bit.

I didn't like lying down and didn't feel well standing up, but I got up. We found my rifle, sunglasses, hat, and also a piece of fallen branch about three feet long and six inches in diameter which had been providentially placed between me and the buffalo in the dusty scuffle. The animal's horns had ripped it almost to shreds. Those goring sweeps were intended for me.

Roger found the missing part of the camouflage shirt. There were teeth marks and a lot of buffalo saliva on it. The buffalo had bitten into the shirt and tore a quarter of it away. I have heard of people being bitten by a frustrated buffalo when it was incapable of doing anything else vindictive. I can only imagine this was occasioned by the long, slow overnight wait. I was thankful it was the shirt, not me.

I lay down and got up several times. We spent some time discussing the matter of getting back to the car.

I talked Roger out of some kind of assistance in getting out. At least I wanted to try it first. My only real problem was a lot of chest pain, a probable consequence of cracked ribs and other damage where I was struck with the horn. We started out slowly.

Getting in and out of little gullies and steeply banked stream beds was difficult, but the longer we walked the better I felt.

We reached the car and rumbled over the road back to camp. There, Harold Padding, with whom we were also hunting, did an excellent job of thoroughly cleaning, disinfecting, and bandaging the wounds. He also treated me with antibiotics, and the healing process went well. Thankfully, I had no aftereffects except for temporary pain and stiffness.

For years I had refused questionable shots when hunting buffalo. Then in a moment of pressure, while I was under the effects of a long, hard run, I yielded and got off a poorly placed shot. I paid for it, but not as dearly as I might have. A good hunter must know when and when not to shoot. I am wiser for my experience. I will ever be indebted to Roger Ingold and even more to God, who gave Roger the presence of mind to handle things just as he did.

# 14

# Mission Mortals

To really need one another as Christians is one of the fine blessings of missionaries in a foreign country, and that applies to missions as well as to missionaries. We often made flights for other missions as several of them had no airplane of their own. It was a valuable service which we could render to them, and it helped us in meeting costs of operation. There were hundreds of flights, but two unusual ones stand out in my mind.

Miss Ruth Utz had been a missionary in northeast Nigeria for over thirty years. She was a concerned and loving person. She had Nigerian children she called her own, not by birth but by adoption. Ruth had grown old. She was well over seventy, retired, but still living in Nigeria. The Nigerian church wanted it that way and so did she. Increased health problems, however, made it advisable for her to be returned to the United States; or so it seemed to the mission. The local Nigerian church did not agree. The mission acquiesced. Time continued to take its toll, and her physical problems were complicated by mental confusion and old-age trauma. The church finally agreed that she be taken back to the United States. Their insistence that she stay in the first place could be misinterpreted by non-Africans. It was not lack of concern for her well-being. It was their custom to care for old people where they felt the old person belonged. But Ruth Utz came to the point where coping with her was very difficult. She had to be taken to the United States for adequate care. The decision to have her returned was made. The problem was to get Ruth to agree.

In the meantime the request had come to us to fly her directly from Biu to Kano where she could be transferred to an international flight. A nurse, Miss Grace Brumbough, was to accompany her. From the description of Ruth's condition, I was greatly encouraged by that news. When the day to pick her up in Biu arrived, we took the rear seats out of the Aztec so she could lie down. We placed a rubber foam mat in the cabin to afford her more comfort.

The Aztec departed from Takum, droned across the Benue valley, over the knife-edged Dadiya ridge, by the appropriate bend in the Gongola river, and an hour and a half later descended toward the almost treeless grassland of the Biu plateau. I always used two converging roads to locate the Biu airstrip, one from the southeast and the other from the southwest. As long as I didn't get on the wrong side of either road I had to arrive over the strip or the town. If visibility was good enough to see the town, which was a few miles due north of the strip, it was not hard to find; otherwise it was often difficult to see the grass strip in grassland.

The Biu airstrip was one of the flattest in the country. It was also smooth except at the beginning of the wet season when, during a short period of time, worm castings were a problem. Landing there then resembled popping popcorn as the worm castings crushed under the tires.

An hour before I arrived Ruth was put into a car under the direction of Mr. Owen Shankster, who had a way of handling her that no one else seemed to have. They drove to the airstrip at Biu, some fifteen miles away.

I landed, taxied toward the parked cars, and stopped, not knowing quite what to expect. The missionaries and some Nigerian church leaders were there with their usual promptness. I stepped down off the wing and Owen Shankster met me close to the plane. He warned me that there might be some explosive words of opposition from Ruth. He explained that she was not accountable for what she said or the attitudes involved. He walked to the car and announced matter of factly that it was time for her to board. He picked her up and carried her to the plane. Silence — baffling silence accompanied the suspense. Grace and I helped Owen put her in the plane. Owen again explained to Ruth where we were going and how much time the flight would take. Grace told her kindly that she would be comfortable and would not have to sit up. But she wouldn't lie down. Instead she sat on the floor with her head just high enough to look out the rear window. We committed her and the flight to the Lord. I started up and taxied out, waiting for something to happen. I applied full throttle, leaving a trail of dust over the runway as we lifted off the airstrip. Ruth simply remained in her uncomfortable sitting position, looking out of the window. Her eyes reflected neither anticipation nor memory, not confusion or comprehension.

For this dear lady, it was the end of an era. I could not help but reflect on all her years of faithful work — and now, this kind of an end to it all. But that was shortsighted and I knew it. Grace, the nurse, was having thoughts as well. Her eyes were moist. Ruth meanwhile resolutely continued to sit up. She did so for the entire trip, not saying a word.

We landed at Kano and taxied to the ramp in the heat of midday. Ruth would not be able to tolerate the routine of a normal check-in. Grace planned to do that for her and for herself as well. Waiting in the heat of the mission airplane for departure time was just as unacceptable. In view of Ruth's unpredictable behavior it was best that she avoid a large number of people. We made our plight known to KLM. A Nigerian KLM employee offered us a Volkswagon bus in which Ruth could wait and rest until boarding time. He showed us where we could park it in the shade. That worked out well.

Later Ruth was put on board the big jet, accompanied by Grace. The huge plane thundered into the air right on schedule, but the departure home for Ruth that day seemed a little "late."

I pondered a number of questions relating to missionaries staying in Africa beyond their years of effective ministry. I concluded that unfortunately there were far more difficult questions than there were simple and satisfactory answers.

On another occasion we were requested to fly an elderly missionary of the Church of the Brethren Mission. She was an unusual person who came to Nigeria as a missionary nurse at retirement age. She made the adjustment well and had a real ministry in the hospital at Lassa in northeast Nigeria. Laura Wine was going strong four years later. She acted and moved about in a way which belied her approaching seventieth birthday. On Sunday, January 19, 1969, however, she experienced back pain which put her to bed, most unusual for her. The symptoms varied in intensity, but were continually evident during the next two days. On Tuesday some strange-looking ulcers appeared toward the back of her throat. Medication was prescribed, and there was no cause for great alarm — yet.

Blood samples were taken and other tests were done by Dr. John Hamer, the missionary doctor at Lassa. Miss Wine's temperature edged upward as she failed to respond to treatment. Her condition would appear to improve and then deteriorate, but by Friday noon Dr. Hamer decided she had to be transferred to the Sudan Interior Mission Hospital in Jos. By then she could hardly swallow, her speech was difficult to understand, and other baffling symptoms had appeared. The medical facilities were far superior in Jos. The problem was getting her there. Travel by road was out of the question.

Before the days of single-side-band transmitters in mission radio in Nigeria, communication was frustrating because the crackling, hissing static often drowned out most of what was said. This was one of those days. Dr. Hamer tried repeatedly to get through to Jos to obtain an airplane from either the Sudan Interior Mission or us. His request was finally understood, but the reply was not. It was not until the next morning that he was assured a plane was coming to get her.

I received the flight request and could work it out with some changes in the schedule which was already set up for that day. Since the most certain thing about the flight schedule was that it would change, we made the adjustments without any fuss. I knew nothing of the gravity of the situation at the time. Only the briefest information came through on the radio and even that was incomplete.

Lassa, where Laura Wine was posted, did not have an airstrip. There was a strip at Mubi, however, fifty miles south of Lassa. The government, due to the civil war in Nigeria at the time, had placed obstacles on the Mubi airstrip; but we were assured they would be removed.

Once the town of Mubi was sighted, the airstrip was not hard to find. I flew east of the town over the airstrip to check if all the intentionally placed obstacles to landing had been removed. They were just rolling off the few remaining empty fifty-gallon drums, but right in the middle of the strip stood an archaic motor-driven cement mixer. The sound and then the appearance of our plane added zest to the job of removal. Several additional people rushed to the aid of the four men who were struggling to push the mixer off the strip. There was no need to delay the landing. With added help, the iron-wheeled monster was ponderously progressing off the side of the runway. I landed, rolled out, and taxied back into my own dust, stopping near the waiting area. The police and security people were there, but there was no sign of Laura Wine. No one had heard anything from Lassa and there was no way to communicate. I walked over to the shelter, talked to the security people — and waited.

Thirty minutes later a Landrover appeared and trundled down the dusty road to the airstrip. Dr. Hamer stepped out and explained that their delayed arrival was due to rough roads and a desperately ill person. They don't mix well, and he was a bit frustrated. He was also concerned because his request for oxygen on board had not gotten through. Additionally, we had the small single engine Comanche, and it was going to be crowded since Laura Wine would have to be in as much of a reclined position as possible. His professionalism far outstripped his frustration, however, and we began to work with what we had. Laura Wine had made it this far over fifty miles of poor road, and the airplane appeared as light at the end of a tunnel.

Time was important. Laura's condition was deteriorating. They had had to use oxygen on the ride from Lassa, so that supply was limited.

I quickly removed two stop bolts which allowed the seat back to tilt down just a little farther. Mrs. Hamer moved into the left side of the rear seat. We placed the partially empty oxygen tank on the floor. We placed Laura Wine, who was quite large, in the seat next to me. Dr. Hamer squeezed in behind and alongside of her, far more conscious of her needs than of his own awkward seating arrangement.

We prayed before we departed. We did so out of custom and out of concern for a very delicate situation. We started up, went through the takeoff check list, taxied to the end of the strip, and departed. I turned to Laura Wine reclined next to me. Dr. and Mrs. Hammer were busy caring for their patient with the meager supply of oxygen remaining. At times Laura's eyes were closed, and then she would abruptly open them. They seemed to be filled with a mixture of gratitude and anxiety. She would open her mouth slightly and move her lips, trying to express herself, but there were no audible words. It is always hard to know just how much attention to give to a patient, especially when they are conscious. In this case, with the doctor on board, she certainly did not need my

help. Patients can be very self-conscious. They can also be encouraged by concern and interest. Treating the individual with a
balance of attention that is sensitive to both needs is appropriate.

We climbed high enough to stay out of low level rough air and
stayed low enough to avoid complicating an already critical oxygen problem. There are not many landmarks flying out of Mubi to
the west until two spectacular peaks in a large rock outcrop about
forty miles west are sighted. These two peaks jut into the heavens
about 2,000 feet and are followed by rolling terrain with scattered
farms. A half-hour later we passed over the dry Gongola riverbed,
leaving the Biu plateau to the north and the Benue valley to the
south. We paralleled the river for about ten minutes and then
passed over the heavily populated area near Gombe. Between
there and the Jos plateau, one hundred fifty miles away, we droned
over the brown uninhabited northern edge of the Yankari game
reserve. I had a constant desire to go faster. Our flying time, as
we passed check points, was actually good, but under the circumstances seemed less than adequate. Conversation was limited. I
gave the doctor periodic estimates for the remaining flight time
so that he could weigh this information against Miss Wine's condition and the remaining contents of the oxygen bottle.

Ground level began to rise below us and the 5,600-foot peaks
to the north of our course came into view. Snaking dry riverbeds,
increasing rockiness, and small bumps in the air all let us know
we were coming closer to the Jos plateau. Finally we descended
over the sloping terrain to the Jos airport. The pressure was mount-
ing to get things done as quickly as possible. The control tower
had relayed by phone my request for the Sudan Interior Mission
ambulance. I had also spoken to the security people via the control tower and received permission to taxi straight to the SIM
hangar. This replaced the usual security check at the control tower.
In view of the critically ill patient on board, I was thankful for
their cooperation. We taxied rapidly, shut down the engine before
arriving in front of the hangar, and braked to a stop while opening
the cabin door. The SIM ambulance was waiting and ready. Within
seconds we began removing Laura Wine from the plane. The process is not quite as simple as it may sound, however, due to the
cramped quarters, the limited access, and a completely immobile
patient. It took a few minutes of positioning people and coordi-
nating physical efforts with a sensitivity to her condition to ac-

_complish the job. With maximum effort and (considering the situation) a minimum of time, she was in the ambulance alive (but in a deepening state of shock) and on her way to the hospital. I watched the departing ambulance rapidly increase speed. I felt concern for the elderly missionary with whom I had such a brief and yet intense encounter. I silently prayed for her and those caring for her. The ambulance passed from sight over the rise.

Of necessity my thoughts turned to such things as adding fuel, filing a flight plan, loading freight, and—I wondered what would happen to Laura Wine.

The following Monday I had a little time in Jos. I went to the Ingolds' home (the Field Director of C.B.M.) to find out how Laura Wine was. She had died the previous evening. Neither Mrs. Ingold nor anyone else knew what disease had snuffed out her life. It was months later, after intensive research and more loss of human life, that a name emerged. Then it became known as the dreaded _Lassa Fever._*

*For the complete story of Lassa fever read the book _Fever_ by John G. Fuller.

# 15

# Internal Affairs

The immaculate, portly African in his long, flowing white robe walked toward me on the parking ramp at the Jos airport. His size and swaggering walk, along with the way in which he tossed the surplus of his robe onto his shoulders, was almost intimidating. He wore a confident expression which he traded for a broad smile as he approached and received my attention.

Normal, rather lengthy greetings were exchanged in Hausa. Then he introudced himself. I was about to receive a request for a flight, and I knew it. The stage was set. It had happened a thousand times. He knew who I was, or he would not have spoken to me in Hausa. The likelihood was that he knew the destination and time of departure of the airplane as well; but to me he was a perfect stranger. The "grapevine" in Africa is very effective.

The request came. He wanted to fly to Wukari. He said that he had heard a few hours earlier that his brother was very ill there, and it was urgent that he go. He asked if there was any possibility of joining the flight. As a matter of procedure I asked if he worked for the mission or the church. If he did, that would automatically make him eligible to fly in our aircraft under government and mission regulations, and there would be no problem. If he did not, the only way we could legally carry him would be without charge. That required a valid reason. He stated honestly that he was not related to our church or mission, nor to any other.

These requests are often complex in terms of relationships, so with a veritable blizzard of thoughts about the legality, propriety, and not least, the Christian attitude and witness involved, I began to formulate a decision. A basic attitude on the part of the pilot comes into play at this point. It comes down to one or two approaches: either help if you can (in any way that is legal, reasonable, and ethical) or don't help if there is any way out of it; and there usually is. The answer is complicated by several factors. An uncontrolled "ride for nothing" approach would lead to an avalanche of requests. At the same time, road travel, while improving, is very time-consuming, as well as hazardous. The string of wrecked, discarded cars and trucks along the roadsides are irrefutable evidence of that. Additionally, the reason (they're not all medical) and truth of the request must be evaluated.

An arbitrary yes or no is not adequate. I began asking questions to get a better picture of the man himself and his request. Then, it is back to the attitude of the pilot. Deep inside I was trying to find a way to either help him or to come up with a reason which would serve as grounds to turn down his request. It is necessary to deal with the matter at its deepest level. A pilot can become either sympathetic or cynical. Dealing with it according to mood can only lead to inconsistent and sometimes ridiculous decisions, which will probably fly in the face of any Christian witness.

I have learned to treat these requests individually and with care. It is much easier just to say yes and get on with the business of the day. When I have done that I have been faced with the "avalanche" I mentioned earlier. To the uninitiated, saying yes or no may seem like a small matter. It is not. The trip may be very important to the person making the request. It might also just be a matter of convenience. In any case, human relations, the pilot's character, and more important a spiritual impact are all hanging in the balance.

Just then the scheduled passengers drove up, and I told the stranger I would get back to him with an answer in just a few minutes. I needed to get out of his presence and think it over. His reason for the request was the one that occurs most often. The problem was that this sick "brother" could mean about anything, both in terms of the extended family and the seriousness of the illness. As in any country of the world, there are people who are straight and others who are opportunists and will say anything to achieve their own ends. Not knowing the man complicated things. Additionally, we would have to leave cargo behind, due to weight limitations, if I was going to carry him. I discarded that. *Things* problems were not to take priority over *people* problems. If the man himself was ill, there would have been no question as it would have come under the medical category.

The two Nigerian passengers that were scheduled on the flight did not know him. Neither did the missionary passengers.

He had moved away from the airplane as I loaded it, standing off by himself. I was uncomfortable with that. I weighed the request again and decided to help him.

I informed my other passengers we would be taking the man and the reasons for doing so. I made the decision to help because to do otherwise accused the man of untruth. It would also have disregarded his concern for a member of his own family. After his rather ostentatious introduction he adopted an attitude of patience. My questions had also revealed facts that were not immediately apparent.

The decision turned out to be the right one. Some are not. There are risks involved. One risk is being "taken" by a smooth talker. The other is the risk of refusing help where it is really needed, and this is much more significant. Part of making right decisions is follow-up. That way a person can learn from mistakes and be thankful for grasped opportunities.

I believe it is essential in dealing with all these requests to begin with the character of Christ, whom we represent. He desired more than anyone in history to help, and His help was balanced by perspective, wisdom, and a deep knowledge of people, their character, and their needs. Then, while all situations will not be handled perfectly by us, if we follow this character we are certainly headed in the right direction.

There is another area of relationships which is significant for any pilot but has special implications for a Christian missions pilot. The relationship is that of the pilot to his environment, especially God's control of the elements. The pilot must have a practical, working approach and a healthy respect for God's natural laws. The line between faith and folly can be obscured unless there are some rather well-defined positions regarding the elements in nature which have the capability of destroying the aircraft and its occupants.

One of those elements, which is peculiar to central and west Africa, is called harmattan. The meteorological term for it is dust haze. It moves down from the Sahara during high winds in the desert. The minute particles of dust form a large mass which drifts to the south and covers huge areas up to a depth of 12,000 feet above sea level. The fine dust is suspended in midair for days on end. It is gray rather than brown. It is not abrasive enough to cause excessive engine wear, but severe harmattan can reduce visibility to a quarter mile or less. It normally occurs in Nigeria between November and March. Its presence can make flying difficult, even impossible at times. The first arrival of harmattan after the wet season (with its good visibilities other than in heavy rain or fog) is always a shock. A week of exposure to it, however, prepares a pilot for the next four or five months when visibilities rarely exceed several miles. Most of the time harmattan is negotiable, but when flying by ground reference points, requires intense attention. There are occasions when it is just less than safe.

The trip had started out with fairly good visibility. I was taking Rev. Ed Smith from Jos to Mubi (about three hundred miles to the east-northeast) for an important church meeting. We climbed to 7,500 feet for smooth air and found it at that altitude. After leaving the eastern edge of the plateau, the ground level dropped to less than a thousand feet about sea level from more than 4,000 feet. Ground contact was no problem. Then a noticeable decrease in visibility occurred over the next fifty miles. I descended to 5,500 and then to 3,500 feet. We passed to the south of the Biu plateau after crossing the Gongola river. Visibility continued to deteriorate. We continued to descend. The terrain at that point begins to rise again. The sun became a silver ball through the dust above. Visibility decreased even more. Finally I said, "Things are getting rather marginal, Ed. We'll continue, but I hope it doesn't get worse."

We had flown a lot of miles together. There was an unspoken agreement that I would do everything I could to get him where he had to go.  He, on the other hand, never called into question any judgment of mine about whether or not to go on.

Several important factors had to be considered. There was no navigation aid at the destination. Mubi was a notorious place for heavy harmattan, and it had steeply rising hills to the east and south, which would require an additional visibility margin for safety.

We bored on. The windshield began to accumulate the light gray dust which further reduced visibility. I was counting the seconds between the time an object came into view and the time we passed over it. I could accurately estimate visibility that way. I began to realize that the flight was probably not going to go on. I searched my mind for alternatives. There were none. It was go to Mubi or go home. I envisioned the solid granite peaks near Pella poking up almost vertically two thousand feet from the surface. I counted seconds again when a large rock formation appeared and rapidly passed under us.

"There is no way to do this one, Ed."

"It's getting much worse, isn't it," he replied.

"We can climb to a safe altitude and go on, but we will never be able to descend at Mubi."

"I understand, Ray." He spoke with resignation in his impeccable British English. We exchanged glances. His sharp eyes, well-spaced beneath bushy eyebrows, often said more than the words he spoke, and now they reflected his audible agreement.

With that I trimmed the Comanche to a climbing attitude and started a turn in the opposite direction. The ground disappeared. We climbed through the dust which clung to everything outside and inside the plane. At about 8,000 feet we reached the top of the layer of harmattan draped over that part of Nigeria. The top formed another well-defined horizon.

It is gray with just a hint of beige. It cuts a straight line horizontally across the blue above. A person feels separated from earth. The sun shown brightly. The danger of low-level flying was gone, but we had not accomplished what we had set out to do.

"I'm very sory about that, Ed," I said apologetically.

"I am sure the Lord has some good purpose in it. We just were not supposed to go. There is really nothing more we can do. I'll send a radio message when we get back to Jos," he said. He always had an appropriate response.

We soared on over the harmattan in the cool clean air above. I reflected on what we were up against. Some elements in nature are immovable and insurmountable. Any degree of wisdom on the part of a pilot dictates a realistic view of that fact. There comes a point when it is necessary to adjust to the conditions because nothing can be done to change those conditions. All that is left to alter is one's own course.

After a half-hour I turned on the ADF (automatic direction finding) receiver and the needle swung toward the Jos beacon. A little later the ground began to come back into view. We descended and landed at Jos.

I always had a paradoxical set of emotions running through me

when the wheels touched the runway after returning due to weather
or operational problems: disappointment in not getting the job
done and yet a sense of satisfaction that we did everything we
could in our effort to get through. It certainly never afforded the
joy of completing a flight to its destination through or around bad
weather. Down deep, however, opting for safety under the pressure of temptation to choose a hazardous continuation of the
flight, always gave me a sense of gratitude to God for the grace
to make that choice.

I described the other silent enemy, called fog, in another chap-
ter. There is also the thunderously loud one. In terms of what
happens inside the pilot's soul, it is also probably one of the most
jarring.

The late afternoon flight from Gboko to Takum was only seventy miles long. We flew it almost daily. The time of year was
early February. The wind had gone from the northeast to the
southwest, but that was not unusual. Harmattan was present which
indicated less than a major change. There were several passengers
on board. Visibility was poor, about a mile, but that was common
for that time of the year. We were fifteen miles out of Takum and
about 1,000 feet above the ground. There had been no variation
in the visibility, no hint of anything different, when suddenly I
began to sense a change in what was ahead. The harmattan-filled
sky was darkening, but it was poorly defined. I descended to have
a better look. We were just passing over Dogon Gawa, rather low,
when it seemed as if a giant hand took the airplane, shook it, and
tried to roll it over. We had run into the severe turbulence ahead
of a thunderstorm which was blocked from view by the harmattan. There was no rain as we hadn't entered the storm yet. The
storms are most violent at the beginning of the wet season, and
I had to back off. I put the airplane into a shallow left turn while
it bounced and bobbed. The temptation was to turn abruptly and
get out as quickly as possible, but a steep bank increased greatly
the probability of the plane going out of control. I fought for
control as the wings dipped steeply, and the airplane was tossed
around in the violent winds. The heading slowly went past north
back toward west. The storm battered us for the last time, and
we were out of its reach. With visibility very poor, no radar, and
impending darkness, there was only one thing to do: return to

Gboko. There was enough light remaining to do that and we did so.

When a flight didn't arrive by a certain time we had automatic radio stand-by times set up. I contacted Lupwe to let them know where we were.

It was just beginning to get light the next morning when Anne was awakened in Lupwe. A man on a bicycle from the village of Dogon Gawa had ridden seventeen miles in the dark to tell her that the airplane must have gone down in the storm the previous day, late in the afternoon. They had seen it struggling in the air and were convinced that it had fallen from the sky. Thankfully Anne could tell him that she had word that everything was all right. The concern and the consideration of the local people was always heartening.

With repeated exposure to communicable diseases, a missionary pilot has to adopt an attitude not only toward the exposure, but also toward the patients as the source of exposure and as people needing help. Handling the leprosy patients, carrying the tuberculosis patient, lifting the meningitis patient, struggling inside the hot cabin of the airplane trying to make the seriously ill patient as comfortable as possible when no one knows what illness he or she might have, has at times raised questions in my mind. On occasion I flew a snake-bite patient or a burn patient with rotting flesh and felt nauseated and totally saturated with the foul odors. I often questioned my concern about self and my hesitation when handling these needy people. I always did what was necessary, but often with at least a feeling of restraint, which in turn gave me guilt feelings. Here were opportunities for concrete expressions of Christian love and concern. Did they have to be accompanied by personal repulsion to the more gross aspects of the disease or accident? While these feelings were not directed toward the patients but rather toward what was wrong with them, I realized that the patients (if they were conscious) or their relatives could only interpret it as a reserved attitude toward helping those who really needed help. My hope was that I was hiding my apprehension. My comfort was that I had less apprehension and greater concern as time went on. I believe that a person needs to do all he can under these critical conditions. They are opportunities, not just duties, to serve mankind and minister to their needs in the name of Christ.

At times the contact gets even closer than anticipated. The Fulani (a tribe primarily engaged in cattle herding) lady had to be placed in the Twin Comanche from the stretcher, which was on the ground next to the aircraft. There was no room for the stretcher in the plane. I picked her up, managed to step up onto the wing, proceeded forward a couple of short steps, and then began to lower her into the fully reclined seat next to the pilot's. In order to do this I had to squat while carrying the patient, and then, with a precarious balancing act, lower the patient carefully onto the seat without falling head first into the aircraft myself. I did lower her into the seat reasonably well, but by then I was totally off balance. This slow-motion scenario finally stopped with my head buried in her lap, my arms pinned rather uselessly under her, and my posterior pointed toward heaven, half inside and half outside the plane door. If it looked half as awkward as it felt, it must have been hilarious. I managed to get my arms from under her, regained my fragile stability, and then proceeded to step carefully over her to get into the pilot's seat. I tried to act as normal as I could, but I really felt silly about the whole thing. I was thankful that in this instance there were only a few people around to see the patient off.

Several days later I had the same challenge at the same place in the same airplane. I was carrying the patient past Marge Kooiman when she glanced at me and smilingly said, "Are you going to do this more gracefully than the last time?" The medical problem was serious or I would have burst out laughing. She had observed the ludicrous situation a few days prior. She had restrained her sense of humor then, and I was obligated to do so now.

At times the Lord presents opportunities to help when they also test priorities. A scheduled flight out of Serti was to go to Wukari and then to Takum. My wife Anne was the only passenger. We left Serti at 6:30 A.M. Ten minutes later we picked up the early morning mission broadcast while in the air. There was a medical emergency at Baissa that had to be dealt with. It wasn't far out of our way. Without hesitation we agreed to pick up the patient enroute. When we arrived we found the patient to be a small eight-year-old boy with meningitis. His back was arched and he was totally rigid. Both his parents wished to go along. Often it is just the mother. The problem here was one of room. We had a scheduled stop to make at Wukari. I could do that as a separate trip, but the rest of the schedule would be thrown off, with the last flight of the day possibly eliminated because of it. So it became a question, not of help to the stricken child and his concerned parents, but of how to work the rest of the day's obligations around that. What goes on mentally at that point can be quite complex. There were a number of people and causes affected. Anne and I talked it over.

We put the boy's parents in the second two seats and laid him across their laps, since he needed to be supported. It was the only way to do it under the circumstances. We loaded their food, cooking pots, ground grain, a few pieces of clothing, a large metal pan (all tied into a cloth bundle), and two cackling chickens into the luggage area behind them. We were trying to accomplish all this and maintain the schedule at the same time. Everything was going well, but the pressure of time was building. The medical advice we received at the strip in Baissa assured us that we could make the stop in Wukari without endangering the boy's life. We looked at the space available, then at the load, and decided that if Anne sat in the baggage area on the little jump seat, we could handle the additional passenger from Wukari, get the job done, and still keep the day's flight schedule intact. At Wukari there was more luggage in other than suitcase form; a few more large pans, another chicken, and some loose things. Our passengers, with the sick child, remained in the plane while we loaded it. Anne fastened her seat belt in the rear of the cramped cabin, and we loaded these articles around her, securing them as best we could. She held several things on her lap. She was practically submersed in assorted cooking ware and flapping chickens. I left the baggage door open until we were totally ready to start up. Closing it, I climbed in the front with the added passenger. Temperatures and stuffiness increased by the second. We prayed, started up, and taxied out as rapidly as possible with the cabin door open. It was hot. Our patient lay rigidly across his calm parent's laps, unaware of what has happening. Lydiya, the added passenger, sitting next to me, was told about the background to the emergency and accepted it as a matter of course. Anne, meanwhile, was in the throes of claustrophobia in the rear of the airplane, but remained silent and resolved. I was unaware of her battle with that problem. Later I was sure I had done the wrong thing by exposing her to that kind of confinement. After closing the cabin door at the end of the strip, we took off and bored through the hot humid air to Takum. It took only twenty minutes, but seemed much longer. We landed and it was a relief to get the door open as we taxied to the hanger. We simultaneously removed the patient and tried to relieve Anne's situation in the back as quickly as possible. The job was done.

The child did well. Dr. Ray Prins, the dentist at Takum Christian Hospital, and I visited him often. His parents were responsive, and we felt that progress was being made spiritually. The boy had, as it were, come back from the dead physically. Eventually he was released from the hospital. We tried to keep contact with the family, but the father, who worked for the government, was transferred to a remote village east of Serti. Two years later we visited the place, but the father had been transferred again. The few Christians in the village said that the father had shown interest, but had not made a definite, personal commitment. We can only hope that where one planted another will someday harvest.

There are some "internal-affair" struggles that seem unending. One of those is the battle of self-control. Part of that has to do with temper, sometimes only felt and at other times expressed. Relentless heat has a way of shortening one's fuse; at least we think it does and use this as an excuse at times. Combine that heat with urgency and deadlines, and the result can be a lot of sweat and fuss.

On one occasion everything was at the ragged edge. So was I. Staff was minimal, added maintenance cropped up, and flight hours were at maximum. In addition, it was one of those hot, muggy days which aggravated anything potentially frustrating.

The young Nigerian woman's hemoglobin was so low that it couldn't be read. Her four-year-old child was ill and badly malnourished. The airplane had been called to take them to the hospital one hundred miles away. An additional sick person arrived at the last minute. A relative usually accompanies the patient to help with food and other things while the person is in the hospital. In this case there were two children in addition to the relative. They obviously couldn't be left behind. I loaded, rearranged, and reloaded everything. Time was pressing. An inordinate amount of it was consumed putting the people and their things on board. Finally, literally dripping with sweat, I slipped into the pilot's seat. The Jibawa lady, who was to accompany one of the patients, sat in the seat next to me. She had a small child in her arms. The two older, but small children were in the seat behind us wailing at the top of their voices. Being strapped into an airplane was frightening. We committed the flight and the people on it to God's care. I am sure He was the only one who heard it in view of all the commotion inside the airplane and the commotion outside as another relative discovered she forgot to send something along. She didn't wait for our prayer to end to excitedly announce it either.

I started the engines with the cabin door open to keep the airplane tolerably cool inside before takeoff. In this case the open door also increased the chaos as the engine noise heightened the fears and the volume of the children's screaming from the seats behind. I quickly shut it while running through the checklist. We bolted down the airstrip, carrying bedlam, sickness, and a highly irate pilot, hoping that somehow he had not shown his feelings. We lifted off, the landing gear was retracted, flaps retracted, 120 mph for climb. We turned on course, climbing between the gigantic hills to the west. The throttles and propeller controls were set. At least we were on the way!

My right hand rested on the throttles. Suddenly I was conscious of something touching and stroking my right forearm. I looked down. My eyes met those of the small child laying across his mother's lap. We were looking at each other "upside down." He grinned widely as he continued his investigation of the hairy arm while he made happy noises, completely resigned to the situation. He had been that way from the beginning, but I hadn't noticed. Then I became aware of the calm and quiet in the back seat. Perhaps it was the motion or the steady drone of the engines, or was it that the tension had been broken? I smiled at the little guy, clad only in beads, and then carried that expression to his mother who had been watching me intently. Her eyes relaxed. She smiled too. Things were still pretty much "upside down" for several people in the airplane, but those dark eyes in that happy little face were telling us something about how to handle it.

# 16

# A Place to Rest

The most certain thing about the flight schedule was that it would change. Today, according to the original schedule, I was supposed to be going west. I wasn't. I was supposed to have a number of dignitaries on board. There were none. I reflected on those changes as we droned on toward Takum over the widely scattered puffy clouds. I glanced behind me to see how my only passenger, Maryamu, was getting along. She was looking out of the window, totally absorbed by the rich green of the Benue valley below and the Cameroun mountains off in the distance. Her beautiful name, derived from the scriptural Mary was given to her at the time of her baptism. She was a beautiful Christian. When one looked at Maryamu, it was necessary to look at more than her appearance to see beauty. Her eyes were calm, but they were built into a swollen face with skin which resembled tightly stretched tissue paper. Her lips were also swollen, but not as much as they were when we flew her several weeks earlier. The white cloth tied over her head partially covered her hair and her ears, neither of which were pretty. Her thin frame was clad in an off-white, full-length wraparound cloth. She weighed very little for an adult. I knew because she needed assistance in boarding. Her hands, at least what was left of her hands, lay across her lap. They had been brutalized over the years. There were no fingers. Scars, depigmentation, and swelling gave these appendages to her arms a useless look. They weren't useless, however, as she used those stumpy hands together like two giant fingers. They were cumbersome, but she was clever — and also ambitious. Her wraparound skirt came to her ankles. She had a huge bandage on one foot instead of a

131

shoe. That foot had become ulcerated again. The other required a modified sandal. There were no toes on either foot.

Living with these problems was "normal" for Maryamu. In addition, she had been sick. That is why we had taken her to the hospital. She had improved a lot and I was taking her home. Home was a leprosy treatment village.

She looked down for a moment and then up at me. Her face brightened. She smiled and started to chatter in her high-pitched voice about all she was seeing out there. She commented about God's great creation.

I marveled at His re-creation — in her.

After arriving at Takum I dropped Maryamu off at her compound in the village which was about a half-mile from our home. We could drive right to her compound. As we approached, people came from their dwellings, and she was welcomed by friends in similar straits. We stopped and with some assistance she got out of the small pickup truck. She thanked me profusely — but I had done so little. I swung the little truck around, drove off between two huge mango trees and back up the stony two-track to Lupwe. Maryamu hobbled off to her small round home. She wouldn't have thought it polite to turn and start off before I left.

As I circled up over the hill and then down the winding "road," I could visualize her frail form sitting stiffly in the plane. By human measurement she would never amount to more than very little. She was poor and needy. But more important she was a sister in Christ. It was a privilege to help her! And if I can say it without the slightest hint of condescension or negation of her person, I felt as though the flight that day had something directly to do with the words of Christ when He said, "I tell you the truth, whatever you did for one of the least of these brothers of mine, you did for me" (Matt. 25:40b, NIV). That is a fundamental part of this ministry.

While the book ends here, the story really doesn't. Unwritten tales unfold every day. Be assured that the kinds of events described in these pages continue to happen, not only in Nigeria, but also in hundreds of other places served by a number of different Christian mission aviation organizations world-wide.